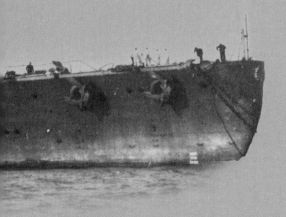

Legends of Warfare
NAVAL

Nagato-Class Battleships
IJN Super-Dreadnoughts *Nagato* and *Mutsu*

HANS LENGERER & LARS AHLBERG

Schiffer
Military History
4880 Lower Valley Road
Atglen, PA 19310

Other Schiffer books by the authors
Akizuki-Class Destroyers: In the Imperial Japanese Navy during World War II, 978-0-7643-6509-6

Kongō-Class Battleships: In the Imperial Japanese Navy in World War II, 978-0-7643-6167-8

Sōryū, Hiryū, and Unryū-Class Aircraft Carriers: In the Imperial Japanese Navy during World War II, 978-0-7643-6077-0

Shōkaku-Class Aircraft Carriers: In the Imperial Japanese Navy during World War II, 978-0-7643-6651-2

Copyright © 2025 by Hans Lengerer and Lars Ahlberg

Library of Congress Control Number: 2025930098

All rights reserved. No part of this work may be reproduced or used in any form or by any means—graphic, electronic, or mechanical, including photocopying or information storage and retrieval systems—without written permission from the publisher.
The scanning, uploading, and distribution of this book or any part thereof via the Internet or any other means without the permission of the publisher is illegal and punishable by law. Please purchase only authorized editions and do not participate in or encourage the electronic piracy of copyrighted materials.
"Schiffer," "Schiffer Publishing, Ltd.," and the pen and inkwell logo are registered trademarks of Schiffer Publishing, Ltd.

Designed by Alexa Harris
Type set in Impact/Universe Lt Sd/Minion Pro

ISBN: 978-0-7643-6965-0
Printed in India
10 9 8 7 6 5 4 3 2 1

Published by Schiffer Publishing, Ltd.
4880 Lower Valley Road
Atglen, PA 19310
Phone: (610) 593-1777; Fax: (610) 593-2002
Email: info@schifferbooks.com
Web: www.schifferbooks.com

For our complete selection of fine books on this and related subjects, please visit our website at www.schifferbooks.com. You may also write for a free catalog.
Schiffer Publishing's titles are available at special discounts for bulk purchases for sales promotions or premiums. Special editions, including personalized covers, corporate imprints, and excerpts, can be created in large quantities for special needs. For more information, contact the publisher.
We are always looking for people to write books on new and related subjects. If you have an idea for a book, please contact us at proposals@schifferbooks.com.

Acknowledgments

In compiling this history of the Nagato-class battleships, we are indebted to the following individuals who over a long time have given invaluable help in our research of the Imperial Japanese Navy: Messrs. Endō Akira, Fujita Takashi, Hayashi Yoshikazu, Ishibashi Takao, Itani Jirō, Iwasaki Yutaka, Izumi Kōzō, Kamakura Takumi, Kimata Jirō, Kitagawa Ken'ichi, Kitamura Kunio, Koike Naohiko, Maejima Hajime, Mizutani Kiyotaka, Morino Tetsuo, Naitō Hatsuho (via Itani), NakagawaTsutomu, Takagi Hiroshi, Takahashi Shigeo, Takasu Kōichi, Tamura Toshio, Todaka Kazushige, Tsuda Fumio, Tsukamoto Hideki, and Tsutsumi Akio.
Special thanks go to Mr. George Richardson for drawings.

All photos are from the authors' collections unless otherwise stated.

Contents

CHAPTER 1	Introduction	004
CHAPTER 2	Design Background	007
CHAPTER 3	The Initial Designs	008
CHAPTER 4	Change of the Fundamental Design	010
CHAPTER 5	Design A 125	013
CHAPTER 6	Building Data and Principal Particulars	015
CHAPTER 7	New Foremast Structure	035
CHAPTER 8	Machinery	038
CHAPTER 9	Armament	045
CHAPTER 10	Protection (Armor and Protective Plating)	073
CHAPTER 11	Complement and Divisional System	077
CHAPTER 12	Principal Items of the Reconstruction	083
CHAPTER 13	Operational Histories	097
CHAPTER 14	Who Designed the Nagato Class?	124
	Endnotes	126

CHAPTER 1
Introduction

It is a well-known fact that the Imperial Japanese Navy (IJN) was built on the model of the Royal Navy (RN) and that with regard to warship construction, the British style was predominant. The IJN's first eight battleships were built in British shipyards, and from 1904 onward, design, construction, and weapon technologies of Messrs. Vickers Ltd. at Barrow-in-Furness were adopted as the standard for Japanese capital ships. This was intensified with the order of the battle cruiser *Kongō* from the said shipbuilder in 1910.

Generally speaking, the construction of the hull, fittings, and most of the equipment, up to and including the battleships of the Ise class, closely resembled the RN standard. But with the Nagato class, the designers turned away from the RN model in some respects and for the first time incorporated several unique ideas. Therefore, these sisters may be considered the beginning of the Japanese-type capital ship and the complete domestic construction of this warship class.

Aside from technical features, this class is also of considerable interest from the politico-military point of view, because the retaining or abolishment of the *Mutsu* caused a big problem at the Washington Arms Limitation Conference. Should the IJN have been forced to abandon *Nagato*'s sister, the resistance of the "hawks" against the Washington Treaty might have escalated into a rebellion.

However, before referring to this aspect, it may first be convenient to outline the key technical features of the Nagato class:

- The world's first adoption of 45-caliber, 41 cm (16.14") main guns in four twin turrets, equally divided fore and aft, with the second and third turrets superimposed.
- The first class of high-speed (or fast) battleships of the IJN built to surpass the British Queen Elizabeth class and in anticipation of the future trend of the United States Navy (USN). An equally important factor for the increased speed was to keep up with the battle cruisers and maintain overwhelming firepower and protection.
- Realization of high speed by the adoption of all-geared turbines and new-type water tube boilers both for oil burning and mixed burning, which was used for the first time in the IJN's capital ships. The machinery generated almost twice the power of the preceding battleships. The arrangement of the engine rooms was unique. The four main turbine sets were situated in three compartments divided longitudinally, with one turbine set each on both sides and two sets in the central compartment. It was expected that in case of damage and flooding, the compartment on either side, of three-shaft operation, could be maintained, and at the same time that list could be

minimized. Vice Admiral Hiraga Yuzuru regarded this arrangement as the most characteristic feature of the Nagato class. This must have been influenced by the British Queen Elizabeth and the Italian Francesco Caracciolo classes.

- A new system of underwater protection was introduced by fitting a longitudinal torpedo bulkhead, consisting of three 25.4 mm thick high-tensile (HT) steel plates, joined together and curved downward from the lower edge of the waterline belt to the double bottom in order to form a protective barrier of the vital parts (magazines and machinery spaces). According to volume 2 of *Kaigun Zōsen Gijutsu Gaiyō* ("Outline of naval shipbuilding technique"), p. 204, this protective method had been experimented with by using a full-sized model, and the result confirmed that it had sufficient strength to withstand the detonation of 200 kg of explosive, predicted at that time to be the bursting charge of future torpedoes.
- Horizontal protection was provided by the middle and lower decks, and both decks sloped downward. The principal protective deck was the middle deck, and the slopes were of the same construction as the longitudinal torpedo bulkhead, and below the waterline it joined the lower end of the lower belt, whose thickness was reduced to 76 mm (from 305 mm).
- Adoption of the concentrated protection system. The length of the waterline belt was reduced to the length of the vital part, and the thin armor above the belt (generally casemate armor) was abolished. The saved weight was used mainly to strengthen the vertical and horizontal protection of the vital part.
- The former tripod foremast was replaced by the "multipost" type and was later extended to the "pagoda style." The central post, with an elevator inside, was supported by six struts to increase rigidity and avoid vibration. Various types of measuring, control, command, and communication equipment were concentrated in the mast, and the trainable rangefinder, of 10 m base length, was installed atop for the first time. This type was adopted only after the construction of *Nagato* had begun.
- The shape of the bow differed from the traditional clipper bow type, used from the battle cruisers of the Tsukuba class to the battleships of the Ise class, the light cruiser *Tone*, and the light cruisers of the Chikuma class, etc. It was rather disadvantageous from the viewpoint of shipbuilding technique and caused splashes on the fo'c'sle, but it permitted the ship sliding over the ropes of the combined mine and became the particular shape of the ships designed for the so-called Eight-Eight Fleet. Also, it provided space for the dignified mounting of the imperial chrysanthemum (1.22 m in diameter).
- Due to the high speed, the mounting of underwater torpedo tubes became difficult, but, on the other hand, the mounting above the waterline was dangerous. In order to gain experience, it was decided to mount half of them below and the other half above the waterline.

From the politico-military standpoint, the following items are most noteworthy:

- *Nagato* and *Mutsu* were the first two battleships of the "dream" Eight-Eight Fleet of the IJN, and the last ones. During the "naval holidays" the IJN built no battleship, so these two ships were recognized as embodying Japan's naval power from the conclusion of the Washington Treaty (February 1922) until the commissioning of the battleship *Yamato* (December 1941).
- *Nagato* was completed in November 1920, and the construction of her sister, *Mutsu*, was accelerated in order to complete her considerably earlier than scheduled. The ensign on *Mutsu* was hoisted in October 1921, just before the opening of the Washington Conference, to pretend completion. But actually, part of the weapons and equipment were not yet mounted, and trials were incomplete. Her condition was debated very severely at the conference and caused a big problem. In the end, the IJN was permitted to retain her but was forced to agree to the continuation of the construction of two battleships of the USN armed with 16" guns (*Colorado* and *Washington*) and the new construction of two British battleships (*Rodney* and *Nelson*) according to the treaty stipulations (35,000 tons standard, 16" guns as maximum).
- The design of the Nagato class was completed and the preparations for the construction had already begun when the Imperial German Navy and the RN fought the biggest sea battle of World War I—Jutland. The lessons drawn from this battle were guiding the design of future capital ships, and all nations tried to implement them as soon as possible. As an ally to Britain and with Japanese observers aboard British warships, the IJN obtained firsthand knowledge. However, the implementation could not be fully realized in *Nagato* due to the preparation stage, but

part of the armor was strengthened and the engine power was increased by a quick change of the design.
- For her sister, *Mutsu*, scheduled to be laid down later, a new design was worked out incorporating in full the "Jutland war lessons." However, the proposed design (A 125) was after all rejected because the construction schedule would have been too much delayed. Had the new design been granted, the *Mutsu* would still have been on the ways at the time of the Washington Conference, and then it is very questionable if the IJN could have obtained permission to complete her without even more serious concessions.
- If *Mutsu* had to be abolished and the possession of the battleship *Settsu* permitted instead, *Nagato*, with 41 cm guns and a high speed of 26.5 knots, would have become a "lone wolf" incapable of forming a tactical unit with the slow and inferior-armed *Settsu*. Therefore, her value would have decreased remarkably, and the probable reaction of the "hawks," as stated earlier, must be considered against this background. As a "dreadnought-type" battleship and hampered additionally by mounting guns of different barrel lengths, *Settsu* was considered useless in the "super-dreadnought" era, and the condition stated above would have resulted in a remarkable decrease of fighting power.

In addition, and referring to personalities, some animosity also appeared between naval architects claiming to be the chief designer or being responsible for revisions and modifications.

CHAPTER 2
Design Background

As a result of the Sino-Japanese (1894–95) and the Russo-Japanese (1904–05) wars and the rivalry between the IJA and the IJN, a coordination of plans was demanded, and on April 4, 1907, the emperor sanctioned a three-part policy document. This document paved the way to the so-called Eight-Eight Fleet, which would comprise eight of the most modern battleships and eight of the most modern armored cruisers (called battle cruisers from 1912 onward). These ships would be in the front line for a maximum of eight years, after which they would be replaced.[1]

However, Japan's naval budgets were very constrained after the Russo-Japanese War, partly because of the great efforts the IJN made in repairing the Russian war prizes, and because of the building costs of new ships.

On July 13, 1911, the Third Anglo-Japanese Alliance Treaty (two years before the expiry of the second) was signed in London, releasing Britain of the obligation to fight on the side of Japan in the event of war between Japan and the United States. Not only did it change the political situation, but it also had a major influence on the armaments planning of the IJN against the primary hypothetical enemy—the United States.

In 1910, the IJN signed a contract with the British Vickers Company for the later battle cruiser *Kongō*. With this order the IJN intended an all-round upgrade of its domestic shipbuilding, engine, and weapon production technology, because at this time, guns over 12" (with mountings), high-quality armor plates, and high-powered and reliable turbines still could not be produced. The most significant item of the order was the dispatch of technicians to perform the technology transfer to the utmost degree. Thus, specialists in each field were sent to Vickers, and besides officers of different branches, engineers, assistant engineers, foremen, and workers were sent. *Kongō*'s three sister ships were built in Japan, and this technology transfer meant that the next generation of battleships could be designed and built in Japan.

However, just before World War I the RN designed and constructed a group of revolutionary battleships that emphasized superior speed, adequate armor, and maximum offensive power—the Queen Elizabeth class. This class would influence the IJN, which after the Russo-Japanese War placed a high value on tactical speed. A speed advantage of 4 knots was seen as a key factor for defeating the USN in a decisive battle.

CHAPTER 3
The Initial Designs

The basic design number of the battleships of the Fusō class was A 64, and that of the modified type, the Ise class, was A 92, completed on June 27, 1914. After that the design of a more powerful class was begun in response to the common trend of the world's naval powers to increase the gunpower, which in turn brought about the necessity to increase the protection and to bring the speed more into line with the battle cruisers. The investigation of the capital ships of ten navies, prominently among Britain, the United States, Italy, France, and Russia, led to the decision to surpass the foreign counterparts both in gunpower and speed and provide corresponding protection.

On September 10, 1915, the new minister of the IJN, Katō Tomosaburō,[1] presented a proposal to the prime minister: the "Supplementary Program for Completion of the Eight-Four Fleet." At a cost of ¥364,291,744 for the financial years 1916–23, four new battleships (*Nagato*, *Mutsu*, *Kaga*, *Tosa*) were to be built in addition to the approved four battleships (*Fusō*, *Yamashiro*, *Ise*, *Hyūga*). A national defense conference (*bōmu kaigi*) was convened to consider Katō's proposal, and on September 13, 1915, it was decided to build one battleship of 32,000 tons (*Nagato*, from 1916 to 1919) and other smaller ships. The emperor gave his approval, and the building program was promulgated on February 24, 1916.

Following the decision of the national defense conference on September 13, 1915, that "the laying down of the other ships should conform to the plan . . . with funding from fiscal year 1917," IJN minister Katō submitted a new armament replenishment plan to the Cabinet. This plan included three battleships to be laid down in 1917, 1918, and 1920, respectively, with completion in 1920, 1921, and 1922, and this was agreed on. This was the "Eight-Four Fleet Completion Program," which was proposed by the IJN minister to the 38th Diet on December 27, 1916. However, the House of Commons was dissolved, but the 39th Diet approved the proposal on June 23, 1917. This enabled three battleships (*Mutsu*, *Kaga*, *Tosa*) and two battle cruisers (*Amagi*, *Akagi*) to be built, and at the end of the financial year 1923 (March 31, 1924), the Eight-Four Fleet was to consist of the following ships:

- eight battleships: *Fusō*, *Yamashiro*, *Ise*, *Hyūga*, *Nagato*, *Mutsu*, *Kaga*, *Tosa*
- four battle cruisers: *Haruna*, *Kirishima*, *Amagi*, *Akagi*

It was initially planned that the Nagato class would be a modified Ise class, with twelve 14", 50-caliber guns of a new type to oppose the latest battleships of the USN or RN battleships, armed with 15", 42-caliber guns. However, Vickers offered a battleship with eight 16", 40-caliber or 45-caliber guns on a displacement of 30,000 tons, and a speed of 25 knots. The IJN also had access to the plans of the Queen Elizabeth class.

Seventeen design studies (A 93 to A 109), including A 102, which is considered the origin of the class, were made and rejected before design A 110 was adopted. The exact date when this design was approved is uncertain, but it must have been drawn up by the spring of 1916, because the Kure Arsenal received the order on May 12, 1916. A further uncertainty is the name of the chief designer. Hiraga Yuzuru was responsible for the modified design (A 112) but not for A 110. However, with a high degree of certainty it can be said that Captain (Shipbuilding)[2] Yamamoto Kaizō was in charge of the design (see chapter 14 for a more thorough discussion).

The planned normal displacement was 32,500 tons. The main armament was eight 40 cm guns arranged in four twin turrets distributed forward and aft. In contrast to the crowded upper and superstructure decks of the Fusō and Ise classes, with their six main gun turrets, these decks were rather spacious and offered considerable space for mounting additional weapons and equipment.

The foremast and mainmast were of the same tripod structure as used in the battle cruisers of the Kongō class. The masts were improved in the Fusō class and further improved in the Ise class. The most characteristic feature, the multipost foremast, was not yet invented.

The 14 cm secondary guns were arranged in two levels on the upper (main) deck and superstructure deck. The above water torpedo tubes were moved up to the upper deck and were trainable.

The armor protection initially resembled that of the Ise class, with a 12" waterline belt and an upper 4" belt. The horizontal protection consisted of 1" plating on the upper deck and 1½" plating on the tripod structure.

With an engine power of 60,000 shp, the speed was calculated to be 24.5 knots.

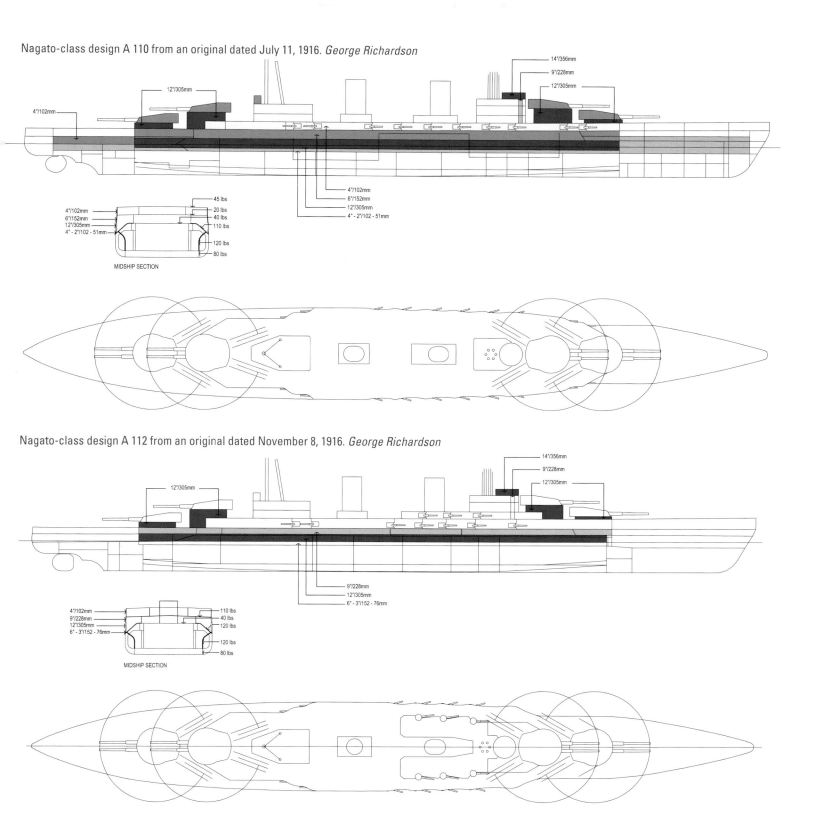

CHAPTER 4
Change of the Fundamental Design

In his lecture to the crown prince, the later Shōwa Tennō, on December 18, 1924, after returning from his visit to European countries and the United States, Rear Admiral Hiraga called himself the "chief designer of the Nagato class," but he entered the Navy Technical Department only on May 15, 1916. However, at the end of this month the Jutland sea battle between the main forces of the British Royal Navy and the Imperial German Navy took place. In this battle, three British battle cruisers were sunk by magazine explosions due to insufficient horizontal protection. After referring to the "Washington Treaty and the Design of Warships," Hiraga elaborated about the capital ships under construction in Britain and the United States and then turned to their protection and summarized the influence of this battle upon the great improvement of the design of the Nagato class.

Like Admiral Sir John Fisher (RN), Hiraga must have considered speed a defensive factor, since the first reference was made to the increase of speed by 2 knots to 26.5 knots by the adoption of all-geared turbines, which, he pointed out, was the "first attempt in big ships." The engine power was increased by 20,000 shp to 80,000 shp, and this 33 percent rise was executed "by the same weight and volume as the result of the big progress in boiler and engine design." Actually, the investigation of the all-geared turbine had begun several months earlier, and the first Nagato-class design had no all-geared turbines (according to Fukui Shizuo, the investigation was started with the goal to adopt this type for the next class of capital ships). The adoption of the all-geared turbine was realized by the investigation of the development of the foreign products at that time and by the import of the technique (and products) of the American Westinghouse Co.

Then he referred to the improvement of the protective power and explained that the length of the waterline belt was reduced at bow and stern, and the upper belt (for protection of the secondary guns) was omitted in order to compensate for the weight increase by the strengthening of the horizontal protection over the vital part (magazines and the machinery spaces).[1] It must be pointed out that the basic structure of the hull and the waterline belt were left as they were,[2] and only the horizontal protection over the vital part was increased. Deck protection was the Achilles' heel of the British battle cruisers, and their decks had been penetrated by projectiles fired from very long ranges when hitting at steep angles. Therefore, the strengthening was the most urgent improvement, in company with fire protection measures inside the barbettes in order to prevent flames from reaching to the magazines.

The Navy Ministry had requested a revision of design A 110 shortly after the Battle of Jutland, and Hiraga stated that by this revision, the weight "of the protective power … increased by 1,300 tons." However, the normal displacement increased by "only" 1,000 tons, to 33,800 tons, so that 300 tons of the weight by which the protection of the vital part was strengthened must have been compensated by the renunciation of armor outside the vital part.

The Navy Technical Department submitted four alternative designs (A–D) in July, of which design C was preferred. Preliminary sketches and a table of the main characteristics were submitted to the Higher Technical Conference on August 30, and after intensive discussions it was approved as design A 112 in September. Kure Arsenal received the order to lay down *Nagato* to the revised design on October 28, 1916.

At that time, the tripod masts were as in the initial design, and it took one more year before the new structure of the foremast was adopted in September 1917, as will be described later.

But design A 112 was not the end. The keel of *Nagato* was laid down on August 28, 1917. The reason for the delay was further studies and revisions of the design drawings. A 110 had been transformed into A 112 in haste, and important changes—particularly of the underwater protection—were required. Hiraga had designed a system with a curved bulkhead composed of high-tensile steel plates, and the changes were so substantial that the design was changed to A 114 on July 27, 1917.

Table 1: Designs A–D

	A	B	C	D
Design guidelines	Speed increase / Defense unchanged	Defense increase / Same speed	Speed increase / Defense increase	Speed increase / Low defense increase
Shp	80.000	60,000	80,000	80,000
Speed (knots)	27	25	26.8	26.9
Protection over secondary guns (mm)	102	0	0	0
Upper belt (mm)	152	254	254	203
Bow and stern protection (mm)	102	51	51	51
Upper deck (mm)	13	70	70	51
Fore part of protective deck (mm)	38	64–38	64–38	64–38
After part of protective deck (mm)	51	102–76	102–76	102–51
Displacement (t)	32,750	32,500	33,800	33,300
Draught (m)	8.9	8.8	9.1	9.0
Additional expenses (¥)	554,644	− 19,613	997,765	782,462
Hull (¥)	54,644	300,387	497,765	282,462
Machinery (¥)	500,000	− 320,000	500,000	500,000

Source:
Ishibashi Takao, *Sekai no Taikan Kyohō* (*The World of the Big Gun Warships' Large Guns*) (Tokyo: Kōjinsha, 2016), 25.

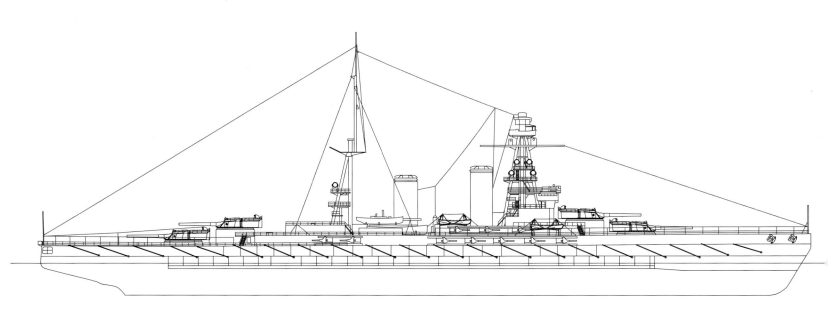

Design A 114 from an original drawing showing *Mutsu* as planned. Note that the torpedo nets were never installed. *George Richardson*

CHAPTER 5
Design A 125

Before continuing with the actual ships built, it might be convenient to briefly discuss the rejected design A 125, often referred to as the *Mutsu Hentai* ("*Mutsu* Variant") design. As mentioned earlier, this design incorporated the lessons learned from the Battle of Jutland. Rear Admiral Hiraga Yuzuru put forward his proposal in June 1917, and his design maintained the same overall length, displacement, and speed as the *Nagato*, but it featured a reinforced armament of ten main guns in five turrets and a significantly enhanced vertical defense through the adoption of inclined (65 degrees to the waterline) armor on the ship's sides.

Moreover, numerous modifications were made, including flattening the ship's hull to secure internal volume, consolidating the main boiler compartments for a revised propulsion system, with a reduction in the number of boilers, and the adoption of a single funnel to accommodate the increased number of turrets. These alterations resulted in a considerable departure from the appearance of the *Nagato*.

Hiraga believed that the "*Mutsu* Variant" could justify a slight increase in budget with its enhanced performance. However, the naval general staff and fleet commanders expressed concerns about potential delays and uncertainties in terms of displacement and construction costs with the adoption of the new design. Consequently, it was rejected.

Furthermore, the decision was likely influenced by the desire during this period to enhance the sustained combat capability of battleships by increasing the number of shells carried per gun. However, the "*Mutsu* Variant," in order to prevent an increase in ship size, reduced the number of shells carried per gun, contradicting the preferences of naval planners.

Hiraga seemed significantly displeased with the rejection of his design, since he even submitted objections to his superiors after the decision was made. Nevertheless, on July 31, 1917, the construction order for the eighth battleship (*Mutsu*) was issued, designating it as the second vessel of the Nagato class.

Table 2: Principal Particulars of A 125 as of June 11, 1917	
Length o.a. (ft.)	708-0
Length p.p. (ft.)	660-7
Beam l.w.l. (ft.)	102-0
Draught (ft.)	27-6
Displacement (tons)	33,800
Shaft horse power	80,000
Speed (knots)	26.5
Armament	
Sannen Shiki 14" guns	10 (5 × 2)
5.5" guns	16 (16 × 1)
3" high-angle guns	4 (4 × 1)
21" submerged TT	4
21" deck TT	4
110 cm searchlights	12
14" shells per gun (normal/full)	80/100
5.5" shells per gun	120
Protection	
Waterline belt (lbs.)	480 VC
Lower waterline belt (lbs.)	120 HT
Upper belt (lbs.)	Included in waterline belt
Barbettes (lbs.)	480 VC to 80 VNC
Conning tower (wall/crown/floor) (lbs.)	560, 440 & 400 VC/280 VC/120 VNC
Lower deck forward (lbs.)	120–100 HT
Middle deck aft (flat/slope) (lbs.)	120 HT/120 VNC + 40 HT
Middle deck amidships over machinery space (flat/slope) (lbs.)	40 HT/120 HT
Middle deck over magazines (flat/slope) (lbs.)	80 HT/120 HT
Deck over side armor (lbs.)	110 HT

Source:
Naitō Hatsuho, *Hiraga Yuzuru Ikō Shū* (*Collection of Posthumous Manuscripts by Hiraga Yuzuru*) (Tokyo: Shuppan Kyōdō-sha, 1985), 238–239.

Notes:
o.a. = Overall; p.p. = Perpendiculars; l.w.l. = Line of waterline; ft. = feet; lbs. = Librae (40 lbs = 1" = 25 mm).
VC = Vickers cemented; VNC = Vickers noncemented; HT = High tensile.
The Sannen Shiki 14" gun was actually the 3 Year Type 41 cm gun.

CHAPTER 6
Building Data and Principal Particulars

The construction of *Nagato* in the building dock of Kure Navy Yard was carried out without any particular technical problems.[1] However, the launching (weight was 22,175 tons) was delayed by almost six months due to difficulties in obtaining materials and the spiraling prices during World War I. But after launching, the construction proceeded at a surprising speed for such a big ship, and *Nagato* was completed in roughly one year. The shipbuilding expenses amounted to ¥15,409,697, and the man-days (per 8.5 working hours) were 1,960,319.

Table 3: Building Data

Item/Name	*Nagato* (temporary No. 7 battleship)	*Mutsu* (temporary No. 8 battleship)
Program	1916 8-4 Fleet Nomination Planning	1917 8-4 Fleet Completion Planning
Budget	Armament Replenishment Expenses (Gunbi Hojū Hi)	
Construction order	May 12, 1916	July 31, 1917
Builder	Kure Naval Arsenal (Kure Kaigun Kōshō)	Yokosuka Naval Arsenal (Yokosuka Kaigun Kōshō)
Laid down	August 28, 1917	June 1, 1918
Launched	November 9, 1919	May 31, 1920
Completed	November 25, 1920	October 24, 1921
Modernization conversion	April 1, 1934–January 31, 1936, Kure Naval Arsenal	September 5, 1934–September 30, 1937, Yokosuka Naval Arsenal
Fate	Survived the Pacific War as the only "operable" battleship. Handed over to the Allied Forces and used for Able and Baker atomic bomb tests at Bikini Atoll. Settled and sank to the bottom of the sea on July 29, 1946.	Blew up at Hashirajima anchorage by magazine explosion (third main gun turret) on June 8, 1943. The Investigation Committee could not clarify the cause that is still uncertain today.
Deleted	September 15, 1945	September 1, 1943

Notes:
(1) The Navy Minister submitted the so-called 8-4 Fleet Nomination Planning, which included the later battleship *Nagato*, to the Defence Conference (*Bōmu Kaigi*) in September 1915 and asked for
(a) Confirmation of the 8-4 Nomination Planning.
(b) Confirmation of the construction of more warships according to the planning of the Navy Ministry from fiscal year 1917 onward.
(2) The Defence Conference confirmed (1a) on September 13, 1915, and also decided to add ¥260,000,000 to the budgets of the fiscal years 1917 to 1923 in order to build eight battleships and two battle cruisers, besides other ships during these fiscal years.
(3) The naval budget for fiscal year 1916 (including the later *Nagato*) was submitted to the 37th Diet session (December 1, 1915–February 28, 1916) and dealt with from January 20 to 22, 1916. The naval authorities asserted, "This planning is based upon the 8-8 Fleet planning. However, the supplementary planning after fiscal year 1917 is the planning of the 8-4 Fleet of the super-dreadnought type ships, with the aim to be completed in fiscal year 1923 and it is not the 8-8 Fleet planning." (The annual shipbuilding planning up to fiscal year 1923 were disclosed in the secret meeting of the Diet on May 29–31, 1916). One part of the planning passed and the ships permitted to be built from fiscal year 1916 onward could be ordered after May 11, 1916—*Nagato* was ordered the next day as shown in the table. Her building expenses were stated as ¥26,920,000 with a displacement of 32,800 tons and ¥841 per ton.
(4) The additional expenses as stated in (b) above were submitted to the 38th Diet session on December 27, 1916, but the Lower House was dismissed on January 25, 1917. Then, the proposal was submitted to the Extraordinary 39th Diet session on June 23, 1917, and passed on July 19, 1917, as the 8-4 Fleet Completion Planning. With this budget the battleships *Mutsu*, *Kaga*, and *Tosa* and the battle cruisers *Amagi* and *Akagi* were laid down. The building expenses of *Mutsu* were the same as for *Nagato*.
(5) Sometimes *Kaigun Kōshō* is translated as Navy Yard.

Table 4: Principal Particulars

Item/Name	Nagato	Mutsu	Nagato	Mutsu
Condition	As completed		After modernization conversion	
Main Dimensions				
Displacement, normal	33,870 (33,800) T	34,116 (34,362) T	39,130 T	
, trial	37,396 T	37,076 T	43,581 (42,700) t	43,439 t
, standard	32,720 T	32,720 T		39,400 T
, full load	40,204 T	39,082 T		
, light load	32,388 T	31,395 T		
Length, overall (m)	215.80	215.798	224.94	224.94
Length, waterline	213.60	213.498 (213.537)	221.07	221.07
Length, between perpendiculars	201.35	201.345	201.35	201.35
Beam, maximum	28.96	28.956	34.59	34.59
Beam, waterline	28.96	28.956	32.46	32.46
Depth (bottom to top fo'c'sle deck)	15.70	15.967	15.70	15.70
Draught, forward		9.001		
, aft		9.157		
, mean		9.079 (9.144)	9.49	
Freeboard, forward		7.925		
, amidships		6.553		
, aft		5.029		
Coefficients				
Block (Cb) (planned values)		0.583 (0.595)	0.5862	
Midship (C⊗)		0.982 (0.984)	0.978	
Prismatic (Cp)		0.604 (0.602)	0.599	
Waterline (Cwl)		0.692 (0.693)	0.667	
Ratios				
Length/Beam (L/B)		7.373 (7.375)	6.39	
Draught/Length (d/L)		0.0415 (0.0428)	0.0427	
Beam/Draught (B/d)		3.189 (3.167)	3.44	
Length/Draught (L/d)		13.6	14.2	
Depth /Draught (D/d)		1.73 (1.72)	1.65	
Tons per cm immersion		44	?	

Sources:

Fukuda Keiji, *Gunkan Kihon Keikaku Shiryō* (*Outline of the Fundamental Design of Warships*), 1, 32; Fukui Shizuo, *Nihon no Gunkan* (*The Japanese Warships*); *Shōwa Zōsen-shi* (*History of Shipbuilding in Shōwa Era*), vol. 1, 435–436, 776, 779; *Weight of Centre of Gravity Data for Miscellaneous Warships* by the Preliminary Design Group (Lieutenant [naval architect] Tōyama, Eng. Imai, Asst. Eng. Takahashi & Ogino) second revision, October 1941; Makino Shigeru & Fukui Shizuo, eds., *Kaigun Zōsen Gijutsu Gaiyō* (*Outline of Naval Shipbuilding Technique*), vols. I, II, and V.

Notes:
(1) Data in parenthesis are planning values depending on Fukuda in case of *Mutsu*.
(2) The bow was of the so-called spoon type (this refers to the slight double curvature with the large cut of the forefoot). This particular bow shape was adopted to permit the ships to slip over the ropes of the connected (or combined mine No. 1–Dai ichi gō renkei kirai). This mine was classified as a military secret (gunki) and many of them were to be laid in front of the approaching enemy force. The bow shape of the Nagato-class was representative for the ships of the so-called 8-8-Fleet.
(3) The appearance of the stern was improved by abolishing the ugly stern walk.
(4) Depth to upper deck 12.805 m; depth to fo'c'sle deck (mean) 14.734 m.
(5) T = English tons (1,016 kg); t = metric tons (1,000 kg). See also Ishibashi Takao, *Senkan • Jun-yōsenkan* (*Battleships & Battle Cruisers*) (Tokyo: Namiki Shobō, 2007), 316.

Table 5: Weights

Condition		As built				As reconstructed			
Ship		Nagato		Mutsu		Nagato		Mutsu	
		(T)	(%)	(T)	(%)	(t)	(%)	(t)	(%)
Hull	Hull	10,148.0	30.0	10,208.6	30.4	11,904	27.9	12,073.8	27.8
	Fittings	1,503.5	4.4	1,280.7	3.8	1,843	4.3	1,620.6	3.7
Protection	Armor	10,361.2	30.6	10,230.8	30.5	8,168	19.1	8,344.9 *	19.2
	Protective plating					6,005	14.1	5,890.6	13.6
Equipment	Permanent equipment	1,051.4	3.1	947.0	2.8	506	1.2	469.8	1.1
	Consumables					523	1.2	534.5	1.2
Armament	Guns	6,184.1	18.3	6,276.6	18.7	6,814	15.9	6,827.1	15.7
	Torpedoes					58	0.1	46.2	0.1
	Electric					513	1.2	545.9	1.3
	Aircraft					52	0.1	50.2	0.1
	Navigation								
	Ammunition								
Machinery	Machinery	3,579.3	10.6	3,435.4	10.2	2,998 **	7.0	3,071.2	7.1
	Oil	500.0	1.5	500.0	1.5	3,000	7.0	3,757.0	8.6
	Coal	500.0	1.5	501.0	1.5	33	0.07	61.0	0.14
	Gasoline					20	0.05	26.0	0.06
	Lubricating oil					31	0.07	78.6	0.18
	Reserve feed water					120	0.3	138.0	0.3
Ballast						162 ***	0.4	159.2 ***	0.4
Unknown		43.2	0.1	198.8	0.6	158	0.4	26.0	0.06
Total		33,870.6	100	33,578.9	100	42,700	100	43,439.4	100

Source:
Ishibashi Takao, *Senkan • Jun-yōsenkan*, 318.

Notes:
(T) = English tons (1,016 kg); (t) = metric tons (1,000 kg)
This table shows the ships as built and in 2/3 trial condition as reconstructed.
* Includes 338 t of barbette armor added later.
** Includes 227 t of boiler water.
*** The water volume in the hydraulic tanks.

The keel-laying ceremony of *Nagato* at Kure Arsenal (*Kōshō*) on August 28, 1917. The photograph was taken just before the chief of the arsenal performed the first riveting ceremony (with the hydraulic machine under the keel blocks) following the Shinto rites. The instruction was given by the commander of the Kure Naval District (*Chinjufu*), Vice Admiral Katō Sadakichi, to the Shipbuilding Section (*Zōsenbu*) staff and executives. In the background on the scaffolding stage are the Kure Naval District commander and his staff; to the right and right rear are the Kure Arsenal's commander, Vice Admiral Itō Otojirō, and various section heads of the arsenal (the head of the Shipbuilding Section is Chief Constructor Captain [Constructor] Nonaka Sueo); and on the lower right of the stage are the Shipbuilding Section members, including Shipbuilding Superintendent Yoshida Yasuzō and Commander (Constructor) Nagamura Kiyoshi.

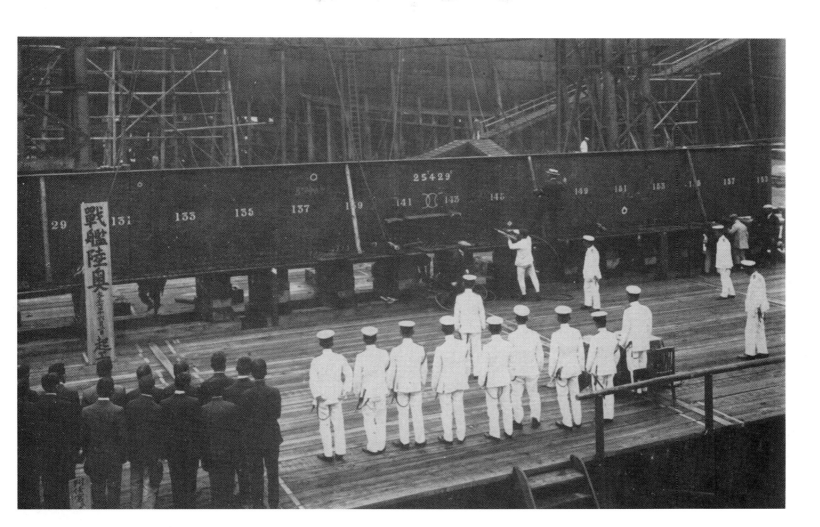

Laying of the keel of the battleship *Mutsu* on June 1, 1918, at the second slipway of the Yokosuka Arsenal. This photo was taken by the yard, and the keel-laying ceremony took place nine months after the keel laying of *Nagato* at Kure Arsenal. The Shinto rituals are completed, and the participants are lined up, with the vertical keel placed on the keel blocks. The rivet supervisor prepared the position for the first rivet (a ceremonial process only) to be driven by the director of the arsenal. The vertical keel number corresponds to the frame number, and the 142nd frame (between 141 and 143) marks the center of the *Mutsu*'s hull (between the forward and aft perpendiculars). The markings on it, consisting of one circle and two semicircles, indicate the midship position. At the right end of the row of naval officers in the second type of military uniform (white summer uniforms), with a desk in front of him, is Vice Admiral Nawa Matahachirō, commander of the Yokosuka Naval District. To his left is the chief of staff, with the three department heads (chief engineer, chief medical officer, and chief paymaster) and staff officers and their aides on the far left. In the middle front of the row of white uniforms is Vice Admiral Tanaka Morihide, director of the arsenal. On the far right of the picture (*to the right of the commander*) is Shipbuilding Section Chief Yamada Saku, constructor general (*zōsen-sōkan*), and Commander (Constructor) Isozaki Seikichi, and in front of him (*in front of the commander*) is Lieutenant Commander (Constructor) Shiraishi Yasutarō. The row of officers in military uniforms to the left includes mainly personnel from the Shipbuilding Section's Hull Factory. Yamada, Isozaki, and Shiraishi all were great contributors to Japan's shipbuilding efforts. Within a few seconds, the director of the arsenal struck the first rivet with a specially made silver hammer, and a skilled riveter completed the first riveting. In the background is the third slipway, where the oiler *Sunosaki* is under construction.

BUILDING DATA AND PRINCIPAL PARTICULARS

Officials at the laying-down ceremony of *Mutsu* on June 1, 1918. *From the left*, Shiraishi Yasutarō (lieutenant commander [constructor]), Watanabe Takeo (sublieutenant [constructor]), Isozaki Seikichi (commander [constructor]), Suzuki Funazo (civilian), Hiraga Yuzuru (captain [constructor]), Kimura Harukichi (civilian), Yamada Saku (constructor general), Masaki Nobutsune (lieutenant [constructor]), Ishiwata Masakichi (civilian), Yasumi Kurakichi (civilian), unknown, Inoyama Tetsujirō (civilian), and Kawahigashi Takushirō (lieutenant commander [constructor], *inset*). Hiraga Archive

Official Yokosuka Arsenal photo of the launching day of *Mutsu* on May 31, 1920, at slipway no. 2. This grand event was included in Japanese school children's reading books from this time until the Pacific War, and all young citizens learned about it.

BUILDING DATA AND PRINCIPAL PARTICULARS

Mutsu fully afloat, but stationary, after being launched. The ship on the port side is the 300-ton *Tugboat No. 4 Yokosuka*. The ship on the starboard bow appears to be the 200-ton *Tugboat No. 3 Yokosuka*, Japan's first experimental diesel ship. The launch weight of *Mutsu* (including the launching cradle) was 16,806 tons, about 2,600 tons more than *Yamashiro*.

The newly completed *Nagato* at Kure in a photo taken at the end of November or early December 1920. The photo was taken by the Kure Arsenal's Shipbuilding Section. The handing-over ceremony was held on December 1, and soon thereafter *Nagato* became the flagship of the 1st Fleet (*Dai 1 Kantai*), flying the flag of the commander in chief of the Combined Fleet (*Rengō Kantai*), Admiral Tochinai Sōjirō, and the admiral's flag can be seen on the mainmast. The photo was probably taken just before the departure to her home port, Yokosuka. Some equipment on the foremast, including the 10 m rangefinder, has still not been installed. The battleship *Ise* can be seen in the background.

The 1st Squadron (*Dai 1 Sentai*) welcoming the Prince of Wales off Yokohama sometime between April 11 and 26, 1922. The Prince of Wales (the future King Edward VIII), who visited Japan aboard the battle cruiser HMS *Renown*, was met by the battleships *Nagato*, *Mutsu*, and *Ise*, shown anchored in that order. At this time, *Nagato* had already been fitted with a smoke cap on the first funnel, while *Mutsu* had not yet completed its installation, distinguishing their appearances.

Mutsu on November 4, 1922, at Sasebo, photographed by Sasebo Arsenal. As a countermeasure to prevent backflow of smoke into the superstructure, a cap or "helmet" (*herumetto*) was fitted to the top of *Nagato*'s forward funnel at Yokosuka Arsenal in early 1922. Although not completely effective, it yielded fairly good results. Therefore, in the autumn of the same year, the same method was applied to *Mutsu* at Sasebo Arsenal. However, the design was improved from the *Nagato*'s cap by creating gaps between the plates, aiming to allow wind to blow through. The photograph shows *Mutsu* at the completion of the forward-funnel modification work. It can be noted that as completed, *Mutsu* had only eight 110 cm searchlights, whereas *Nagato* had ten. The searchlights were of the Sperry type (*SU shiki*), but starting in 1933 this type was replaced with the type 92 (*92 shiki*).

Nagato with a smoke cap on the forward funnel about 1923. This measure was taken to reduce the negative effects of soot and smoke on the foremast, but it was not very effective. Later, the funnel was significantly bent backward. Two 8 cm single high-angle guns covered with white canvas can be seen next to the funnel.

Nagato during the summer tactical training (*sengi kunren*) of 1924, photographed in August 1924. A balloon can be seen in the upper right of the picture; this was used for artillery spotting and had been carried on board since late 1922.

Mutsu probably departing for or returning from a training exercise, because she appears to tow a target raft from the stern. A cap is fitted on the forward funnel, which was part of the construction work that started in November of the year following *Mutsu*'s completion and was finished by March 1923. From the time of completion, *Mutsu* was not fitted with side-mounted torpedo nets (*bōgyomō*), and the configuration of the forward superstructure was slightly different from that of *Nagato*, with a new bridge command station (*shirei-sho*). Additionally, the position of the Imperial Crest on the bow was placed higher than on *Nagato*.

Mutsu at anchor about 1924. The forward funnel has been modified, but the bow is still not altered. Even before the modification of the bow, the position of the Imperial Crest (*Gomonshō*) (chrysanthemum) differed slightly from that of *Nagato*, and the shape of the fairleads nearby was also different. The balloon raised at the stern is another feature of this period, used for spotting the fall of shot. This was especially important for this class of ship, which had a long firing range.

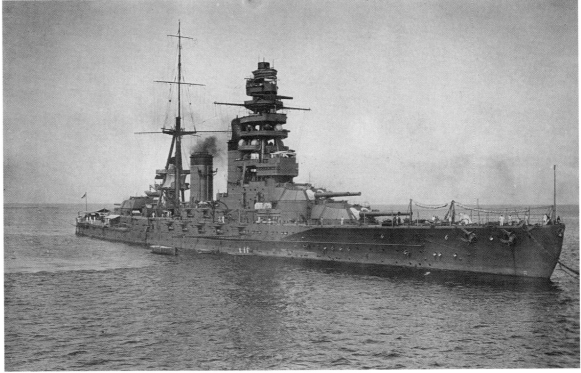

Nagato at Yokosuka around the autumn of 1924. Originally, *Nagato* had two searchlights on the upper part one deck below the 10 m rangefinder, but here the searchlights have been removed and replaced with a target survey station (*sokuteki-sho*). Additionally, a new rangefinder for the secondary guns has been installed on the compass bridge (*rashin kankyō*).

Nagato with the bent-forward funnel photographed in March–April 1925, at Yokosuka. This photo shows the ship shortly before departure for Tateyama Bay for a hands-on observation tour by many students from the Army Cadet School, right after the completion of work to modify the forward funnel. That year, the ship was a training vessel for the Naval Gunnery School (*Hōjutsu Gakkō*). A searchlight platform, with a 110 cm searchlight, was installed on the port side of the forward funnel for experiments to prevent bridge glare, improve illumination effectiveness, and assess the impact of hot smoke. The platform was removed about two months later. Note the deflection teacher (*shōjun-enshūki*) fitted on turret 2, a device invented by Admiral Sir Percy Scott, RN, used to improve the training of guns onto a target.

Mutsu with a captive balloon (*keiryū-kikyū*) under maintenance, photographed in the late Taishō period about 1925. It is a somewhat unusual sight, showing a captive balloon being maintained on the aft deck. The Imperial Japanese Navy introduced these balloons from Britain in 1918, and they were installed on *Mutsu* starting in July 1922. They were used for spotting the fall of shot (*danchaku kansoku*) during long-range gunnery and for monitoring the tracks of launched torpedoes. Unfortunately, the maneuvering of the ship while towing the balloon posed significant challenges. In 1926 these balloons were removed.

Mutsu at Sasebo in May 1925. This image shows *Mutsu* as the flagship of the Combined Fleet, viewed directly from the bow during a gun drill (*sōhō kunren*). The ship is anchored using a buoy with the starboard anchor chain extended, and the lower booms on both sides are bustling with traffic boats and tenders. Notably, the yardarms on the upper part of the foremast extend backward on *Mutsu*, whereas on *Nagato*, they extend at right angles. *Sekai no Kansen*

Mutsu anchored at Sasebo on May 28, 1925. This is after the bending modification of the forward funnel, which was carried out at Sasebo in March 1924, ahead of similar work on *Nagato*. The shape of the support struts for the bend is different from those on *Nagato*, and it appears that the installation of 8 cm antiaircraft guns was not carried out on *Mutsu*. During this period, the form of the foremast differed somewhat from that of *Nagato*. The 3.5 m rangefinders on the bridge are at different heights (whereas they are at the same height on *Nagato*), and the shape of the bulwark in that vicinity also shows significant differences.

Mutsu on May 28, 1927, at Sasebo after the bow modification. As seen in photos from the original full-power trials, the upper part of the bow of the Nagato class was wide, causing heavy spray to be thrown up in rough seas, affecting the bridge and turret rangefinders. To address this, *Mutsu*'s bow was modified as shown here. Note that the portside 3.5 m rangefinder on the compass bridge (*rashin kankyō*) is placed higher than the starboard one. *Nagato*'s rangefinders were placed at the same height on both sides. In 1927, *Mutsu* was part of the 1st Squadron along with *Nagato* (flagship), *Ise*, and *Hyūga*. After cruising to northern China, she returned to her home port, where the modification was carried out in a short period. The new painted section visible at the bow tip marks the modified area. Although this modification was effective, it was still insufficient, and *Nagato* was not modified for several more years. By 1927, the Nagato class had already been equipped with reconnaissance seaplanes, with a hoisting derrick installed on the starboard side of the aft superstructure. The Nagato class was very stable in all planned firing arcs, something that was very important in long-range gun battles.

Mutsu at anchor around 1928. It seems to be a scene from a gun drill (*sōhō kunren*), with the second turret trained aft to starboard and the third turret trained forward to port. Although it is difficult to see in the photograph, the shape of the support structure for the bent-forward funnel and the steam exhaust pipes running alongside it differ between *Mutsu* and *Nagato*.

View of *Mutsu* from the bow in 1927–29. Note the position of the Imperial Crest (*Gomonshō*).

Mutsu as seen from the stern. This image likely depicts *Mutsu* in the early Shōwa period around 1927–29, as evidenced by the installed facilities for carrying reconnaissance seaplanes. Although the beam of *Mutsu*'s hull was increased by only 1 foot (30 cm) compared with the previous Ise-class battleships, the ship appears very robust and solid when viewed from this angle.

Bow view of *Nagato* in October 1930. The freeboard forward was 7.9 m at the bow, 5 m at the midsection of the ship, and 4.85 m at the stern. At full power with a rudder angle of 35 degrees, the turning radius was within two to three times the ship's length, which was better than the Ise and Kongō classes. The ships had two anchors on the starboard side and one to port. Later, one anchor on the starboard side was removed.

Mutsu as flagship of the Combined Fleet on a photo taken probably a few days before the grand naval review (*daikankanshiki*) at Kōbe on October 26, 1930, by Utsunomiya Shōten. *Mutsu* is seen carrying two type 14 Reconnaissance Seaplanes (*14 Shiki Suitei*) between the aft bridge and the third turret, with one plane having its wings folded. The reinforcement at the attachment point of the aircraft derrick on the starboard side of the mainmast is notable. The ship's exterior, soiled from extensive exercises, has been completely repainted. Many crew members in full uniform are lined up on the main and upper decks, possibly for a divisional inspection (*buntai tenken*) or another event. The Rokkō mountain range is visible in the background.

CHAPTER 7
New Foremast Structure

The initial design of the Nagato class had the same type of tripod masts as in the Ise class. When *Nagato* was laid down in August 1917, *Ise* and *Hyūga* were in the fitting-out stage and almost completed (December 1917 and April 1918, respectively). Therefore, if *Nagato* had adopted the multipost-type foremast at the time of approval of the revised fundamental design (October 1916), the design of the Ise class would have been changed to adopt this type too. With this argument, the late Fukui Shizuo explained that the multipost foremast was adopted by changing the design during construction. He continued that this idea was proposed by the then captain (later vice admiral) Kaneda Hidetarō, who asserted the adoption very strongly and added that he heard this directly from Commander (later vice admiral) Hiraga, then in charge of the procedure. By the way, Kaneda was no technical officer (*gijutsu shōkō*), but a line naval officer (*heika shōkō*, graduate of the naval academy).[1]

The purpose of this mast structure was (1) to prevent vibrations, which so remarkably influenced the accuracy of targeting, measuring, spotting, and other highly sensitive instruments, and (2) to permit the continuation of measuring and fire control even in case of firing. The 40 cm guns of the Nagato class had a greater range than the 36 cm guns of the predecessors; engagement ranges in World War I were much greater than expected, and at these ranges the effect of the main guns depended on the quality of the fire control system (i.e., the capability to hit first and keep hitting).

The most important presupposition to attain this goal was to provide a very rigid platform for mounting these instruments high up. Increased ranges required higher positions for the optical instruments; otherwise, the enemy could not be observed and would remain behind the horizon due to the earth's curvature. An enemy vessel that had its rangefinders and other optical instruments mounted high would have the advantage and would outrange its opponent—a situation that had to be prevented at all costs.

The modifications of the tripod mast realized in the preceding classes had not brought about expected results; therefore the solution must be a revised structure. Kaneda's multipost mast was composed of a central post of large diameter surrounded by eight equally spaced and inclined support struts, combined with the central post high above the waterline. This structure was more rigid than the tripod mast and was very stable, so that vibrations, as in case of the former mast structure, could be avoided and a steady platform for the various conning stations and equipment could be attained.

Three months after *Nagato* was laid down, the technical conference (*gijutsu kaigi*) of the Navy Technical Department was held on November 21, 1917. The principal theme was Kaneda's invention. "Heated arguments" were again exchanged, but finally the adoption was decided. However, the weight remarkably exceeded that of the tripod mast and influenced stability. This being Hiraga's main argument, he accepted the structure only after reducing the number of support struts from eight to six. Even though this meant a reduction of rigidity, he evaluated the influence of weight in high position upon stability higher.

In its final form, the mast was composed of the main post, 1.9 m in diameter (fitted with an elevator inside, connecting the middle deck with the battle bridge), surrounded by six inclined support struts of 0.91 m diameter (arranged every 60 degrees around the circumference) and combined at the upper end to form a conical type of mast. At the lower part, bridges merged with the mast components. At each flat above, searchlights and other equipment were fitted, and the upper-part structures with fire control and range-measuring installations again merged with the mast components. Therefore, the hexagonal structure and the main post could be recognized only in the middle part. It was called *yagura* (pagoda) style and was the origin of the pagoda-type mast, which became a characteristic feature of the Japanese battleships, before changing to the tower-type foremast of the Yamato class. The height from the upper deck to the top was fourteen floors.

Even before the modernization conversion, the appearance of the mast changed by mounting new weapons and fittings or shifting to other positions. After the modernization conversion, the shape differed remarkably from before, but even after that there were revisions.

Nagato during fitting-out work in 1920. The ship had been laid down at Kure Arsenal on August 28, 1917, and was launched on November 9, 1919. The photograph shows the structure of the foremast, consisting of seven pillars (including the main post). Incidentally, this foremast design was proposed by then commander Kaneda Hidetarō, known for his 500,000-ton battleship plan, and it became a common design for the main battleships that constituted the later Eight-Eight Fleet. *Sekai no Kansen*

Above: *Nagato* at Hakodate about 1921. Note the missing 10 m rangefinder and the peculiar bow type. The spoon (*supūn*) type of bow was adopted in order to enable the ship to pass over the linked floating mines (no. 1 mines [*1 Gō kirai*]), planned to be used during the fleet's decisive battle. However, there were problems with the bow's seaworthiness. In this photo it can be seen that the torpedo nets have already been removed.

Right: *Mutsu* in dock for trials at Yokosuka Arsenal Dock No. 5 on September 20, 1921. *Mutsu* had sailed from Sasebo to Yokosuka to be docked. Although many parts are still incomplete, the handover ceremony was conducted on October 24, to hasten completion due to the implications of the Washington Disarmament Conference. Because of the limited time, various compromises were made, such as using substitute materials with inferior capabilities for the vertical and horizontal armor. The naval ensign was hoisted, and the remaining work was carried out, with the ship being practically completed by November 23.

CHAPTER 8
Machinery [1]

The machinery adopted for *Nagato* is of particular interest for three reasons:

- Geared turbines were adopted for the first time in a major IJN warship.
- The turbines were designed independently by the Design Group of No. 5 Division of the *Kaigun Gijutsu Honbu*,[2] using the revolutionary triple-flow-turbine concept developed by the American Westinghouse Company.
- The reduction gearing for *Nagato* was purchased directly from Westinghouse, but the gearing for her sister, *Mutsu*, was manufactured under license by Yokosuka Navy Yard, using a hobbing machine purchased from the US company.

The steam for the operation of the main turbines and the greater part of the auxiliary machinery was provided by fifteen *Ro Gō* Kampon-type oil-burning boilers, with superheaters generating saturated steam, and six mixed-burning boilers, twenty-one boilers in total.[3] There were animated discussions about the continued use of boilers with mixed firing alongside boilers fired exclusively by oil, but the debate was concluded by the head of No. 5 Division, who argued that coal firing was still necessary due to the high cost of imported heavy oil. The designed maximum power was 80,000 shp.

The main turbines were four sets of Gihon all-geared impulse-type turbines, each consisting of one high-pressure turbine (HPT) and one low-pressure turbine (LPT). What made them of particular interest is that these turbines were designed in the fashion of the American Westinghouse triple-flow system and were the beginning of the so-called double-flow system, without fitting the cruising turbine stages. The steam passed through the first impulse stage in the HPT and was then divided into three parts. One part went to the group of rotor blades in the HPT casing, and the other two entered the casing of the LPT in the center, where they were divided into the forward and aft direction to pass the two groups of rotor blades in the opposite directions. By bypassing these three groups (one in the HPT and two in the LPT), economy of the steam at low speeds was attained. When the ship was steaming at cruise speed, the flow of steam to the LPT was cut off, and only the HPT operated. There was no cruise stage in the main turbines, nor was there a separate cruise turbine.

The turbine blades were the Gihon type, developed by the IJN from the Brown-Curtis system, and this type was the origin of the later Kampon-type blades.

The primary aim of the triple-flow system was to reduce steam (and hence fuel) consumption, but results proved disappointing. A peculiarity of these ships was the mounting of synchronous speed when cruising on the wing shafts in order to eliminate "drag" when the shafts were feathered.

Reduction gearing allowed the adoption of lightweight, fast-running turbines. The speed of both turbines was 2,731 rpm, and the maximum designed rpm of the four propeller shafts was 230.

The reduction gears for *Nagato* were produced by the American Westinghouse Company.[4] They were a new attempt at using a "floating frame" for support of their pinions, with the hydraulic type for *Nagato* and the I-beam type for *Mutsu*.[5]

The wheel had 392 teeth cut with 30 degrees of helical angle, and each pinion had thirty-three teeth. There was no difference between the HPT and LPT gearing.

The reduction gearing fitted in destroyers of the US Navy generated much noise, and after the fitting in *Nagato*, particular attention was given to this phenomenon, but no particular noise occurred.

The weight of one set of Gihon turbines was 50.8 tons, that of the reduction gearing 54 tons, making a total of 419.2 tons for all turbines. This means that 190.8 shp per ton was developed. A remarkable achievement compared with 53.3 shp/ton for *Fusō* and 56.1 shp/ton for *Hyūga*, both of which had conventional "heavy," slow-running direct-drive turbines.

The diameter of the four three-bladed propellers was 4,191 mm, and pitch was 4,407 mm. Two rudders of balanced type were fitted.

With 3,400 tons of heavy oil and 1,600 tons of coal, 5,500 miles at 16 knots could be attained.

Electricity was provided by four 250 kW turbogenerators (1,110 A), two 150 kW reciprocating generators (667 A), and one 26 kW semidiesel generator (115 A), to make a total of 1,026 kW. Voltage was 225 V, current type DC.

The next table shows the engine room and boiler room spaces as built and after the modernization conversion. In contrast to the other capital ships, the Nagato class did not change the turbines—only the boilers. Due to the progress of boiler technique, the area could be reduced by almost 200 m² without loss of power.

Table 6: Machinery Spaces

Item	Engine rooms		Boiler rooms	
Condition	As built	After modernization	As built	After modernization
Shp/boiler	81,300	82,300	15 oil, 6 mixed	Oil, 4 large, 6 small
Length (m)	26.82	26.82	49.680	39.014
Width (m)	19.34	21.55	16.610	16.610
Heigh (m)	9.448	9.448	8.534	8.534
Floor area (m²)	516.20	519.25	825.30	648.09
Shp/m²	157.5	158.5	98.5	127.0

Source:
Fukuda, op. cit., 147.

Table 7: Trial Results

Ship		Trial displacement (tons)	Speed (knots)	Output (shp)	Propeller shaft speed (rpm)	Execution Location	Date
As built	Nagato	33.759	26.44	85.478	234.6	Sata-misaki	6 Oct 1920
	Mutsu	33,750	26.73	87,494	230.6	Uraga Suidō	19 Oct 1921
As reconstructed	Nagato	43,473	24.98	83,445	223.0	Sata-misaki	17 Dec 1935
	Mutsu	43,496	25.28	82,578	222.0	Uraga Suidō	27 Jul 1936

Source:
Abe Yasuo, *Sekai no Kansen* 854, 120.

Table 8: Turning

Name	Nagato	
Item/Condition	As built	After conversion
Displacement	33,820	43,861
Speed (V)	24.9	24.0
Ar (rudder area)	60.0	55.6
Am/Ar	32.59	34.98
DT/L	2.33	2.20
Heel angle	11°5'	10°5'

Source:
Fukuda op. cit., 124

Notes:
Ar = rudder area (m²); Am = lateral middle line area (m²); DT = transfer

Machinery layout of the Nagato class. *Sekai no Kansen*

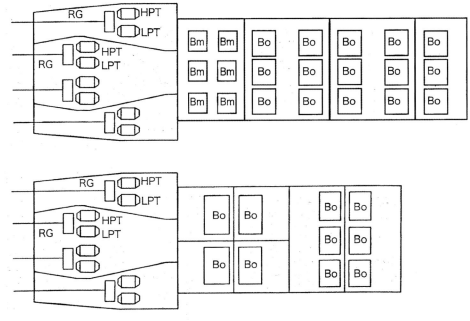

Machinery layout as built (upper) and after reconstruction (lower)

HPT = HP turbine; LPT = LP turbine; RG = Reduction gearing; Bo = Boiler oil fired; Bm = Boiler mixed firing

Turbine layout. *Sekai no Kansen*

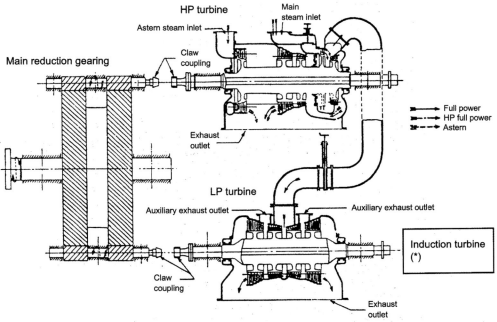

Layout of turbine set - port side forward as built

* During reconstruction induction turbine was attached to the outer shaft's LP turbine via reduction gearboxes and coupling devices

MACHINERY 41

Floating pinion cradles. *Courtesy of Takagi Hiroshi*

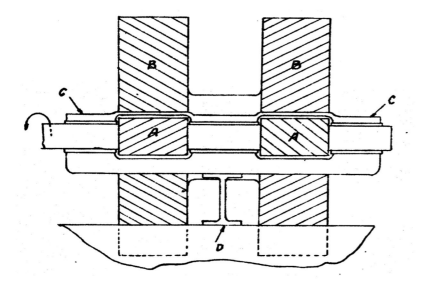

Floating Pinion Cradle (I-beam Support)
A = Pinion; B = Gear; C = Floating frame (cradle); D = I-beam (flexible)

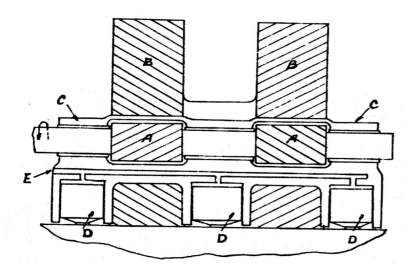

Floating Pinion Cradle (Hydraulic Support)
A = Pinion; B = Gear; C = Floating frame (cradle);
D = Hydraulic piston; E = Communication oil path

The newly built *Nagato* undergoing final full-power trials on October 27, 1920. This impressive image was published by the Navy Ministry simultaneously with the completion of the ship. During this trial, the ship recorded an output of 85,500 shp and a speed of 26.7 knots. The main guns, positioned in a superimposed configuration forward and aft, are 41 cm, 45-caliber twin guns. At the time of construction, the maximum elevation was 30 degrees, and the maximum range was 32,500 m.

Nagato during full-power trials in Sukumo Bay on October 27, 1920. Although the 10 m rangefinder on the foremast was not yet installed, the ship was handed over to the navy on November 25. The forward funnel was close to the foremast, causing the exhaust to flow back toward the foremast. This led to issues such as the upper part becoming very hot and negatively affecting the accuracy of the rangefinder. The Nagato class had excellent acceleration, and maneuvering capabilities second only to the battle cruisers of the Kongō class. *Sekai no Kansen*

Mutsu during full-power trials off Tateyama on October 19, 1921. Unlike the Fusō- and Ise-class battleships, this class is known for being the first Japanese battleships to adopt a thoroughly concentrated defense system. Before the construction of *Mutsu*, an alternative design known as the "*Mutsu* Variant" (A 125) was considered. This plan proposed adding an extra main gun turret and adopting inclined side armor to enhance offensive and defensive capabilities, but it was not adopted due to various circumstances. To ensure the ship was completed before the Washington Naval Conference, the construction of *Mutsu* was rushed and officially completed on October 24, 1921. However, many parts were still unfinished, and the main gun trials were conducted at the beginning of the following year. Note that the main and secondary guns did not have waterproof covers when newly built.

Mutsu during trials between the pillars off Tateyama on October 19, 1921. At this time, the ship had a displacement of 33,750 tons, and with 87,494.4 shp she achieved 26.728 knots. *Mutsu* differed from *Nagato* in several aspects: the shape of the blast screens (*bakufū yoke sukurīn*) at the base of the foremast had a different shape, and the placement of the command station (*shirei-sho*) below the rangefinder atop the foremast had two fewer searchlights on *Mutsu*. Another difference was that *Mutsu* had 8 m *Bu*-type rangefinders on her main gun turrets.

CHAPTER 9
Armament

Main Guns

The adoption of the 16" (406.4 mm) gun as the main gun to be mounted on the next class of battleships after the Fusō class[1] had been under investigation since 1913. At that time, the mounting of 15" (381 mm) guns on the newly designed British fast battleships of the Queen Elizabeth class was an acknowledged fact, and the mounting of 16" guns on American battleships was considered to be only a matter of time. However, the details of the larger-caliber gun were not certain, and the increase from 14" (355.6 mm) to 16" was a remarkable challenge from the technical point of view. Therefore, a comparative investigation of the 15" gun, already produced in Britain, and the proposed 16" gun was decided in order to make a decision.

The principal key questions were

- length of 40 or 45 calibers?
- effect of fire and weight of projectile?
- caliber 15" (381 mm) or 16" (406.4 mm)?

The ballistic requirements were a projectile velocity of 580 m/second at a range of 8,000 m, with a maximum barrel pressure of 29.33 kg/cm^2.

The advantages of the 40-caliber gun, such as shorter barrel length, less vibration, slightly smaller dimensions of the turret and roller path diameter, and less weight, were the disadvantages of the 45-caliber gun. But the advantages of the latter, such as smaller powder chamber, less erosion and, hence, longer life of the gun, and longer firing range were considered to surpass the disadvantages. Thus, the adoption of 45-caliber length was proposed and accepted.

As for the projectile, three types were investigated (see table 9).

Table 9: Investigated Projectiles		
Type (mm)	381	406.4
Light weight (kg)	780	948
Intermediate weight (kg)	825	1,002
Heavy weight (kg)	948	1,061

The lighter the projectile, the smaller the powder chamber and the less the erosion. However, the weight also influenced the penetration power, and if the lightweight projectile was adopted, there was not much room for improvement should a higher muzzle velocity be required in the future. The heavy projectile brought about almost contrary results. In the end, the adoption of the intermediate weight projectile was proposed

When comparing the calibers, the superior penetration, larger bursting charge (hence, greater destructive power), and longer firing range again outweighed the disadvantages as stated above (heavier weight, longer gun, more erosion).

In the end, the advantages of a larger caliber led to the decision to adopt this gun for the next class of battleships, in order to, again, put the IJN ahead of the other major powers, as had been the case when the IJN adopted the 14" gun for the Kongō class.

According to Horikawa Kazuo & Ondo Shinsaku in their *Notes on the History of the Former Military Steel Technology*, the "lightweight" trial 16" gun was completed in 1914 and was "mass-produced" as the 45-caliber Three Year Type 41 cm Model II gun, with some changes compared with the trial gun (some fundamental data are shown in parenthesis in Table 10).

	Table 10: Main Guns
Item / Type	45 cal Three Year type 41 cm gun Model II (Trial gun)
Caliber, nominal/actual	40 cm/410 mm (16.14")* (406.4 mm)
Barrel length, breech face to muzzle (m)	18.294
, overall (m)/in calibers	18,840/45.95 (18.840/46.4)
Length from shell base to muzzle (m)	15.8621
Length of rifling (m)	15.844
Length of wire wound part (m)	15.629
Center of gravity (from breech face) (m)	5.8772
Length of the screw box (mm)	380
Length screw box to shell bottom (m)	2.5979
Length breech face to shell base (m)	2.9779
Weight including breech mechanism (tons)	102 (113.456)
Construction	Wire-wound, four layers at muzzle and breech
Breech	In contrast to the cylindrical interrupted screw breech of Vickers type, the fore and aft parts of the Type 41 were inclined 5° to make opening and closing easier. Seen from the side the middle part appeared like a bulge. Invented by the later Vice-Admiral (weapon production) Dr. Arisaka Shōzō, the adoption of this breech was officially announced on August 21, 1908, and was used from 8 cm guns upward for nearly all Japanese naval guns as the Type 41 (1908) breech.
No. of grooves/depth and width (mm)	84/4.1 × 8.754 (96)
Twist	uniform (1 in 28 cal.)
Bore cross section (cm^2)	1,347
Chamber, length (m)	2.3204**
, diameter (mm)	440 aft, 513.8 center (512 center)
, volume (liters)	467.07**
Total content of the gun barrel (liters)	2,616.94
Relation total content barrel/chamber volume	5.4491
Powder container	4 bags (1/4 charges) of 55.5 kg
Muzzle velocity; designed/actual (m/s)	780/805*** (850)
Maximum bore pressure (bar)	30.0–30.7
Muzzle pressure (bar)	5.4
Projectile weight (kg)	1,020 (Type 91 AP, TP) + (1,000) 936 (CS, IS)
Charge weight (kg)	222++ (also 219 are given) (245)
Ignition weight (kg)	1.0
Projectile travel (m)	15.974 (Type 91 AP shell)
Point of complete combustion	20 cal from muzzle
Maximum range, horizontal/vertical (m)	30,200 (at 30°) 38,300/11,100 (at 43°)
Approximate life	250 rounds+++

Notes:
By Navy Order No. 9 on March 29, 1922, the designation of the gun was changed to 45 Caliber 3 Year Type 40 cm Gun (45 Kōkei 3 Nen Shiki 40 senchi Hō).
* The first official caliber was 41 cm but this was changed to 40 cm. Most probably by considering the influence upon foreign navies because it exceeded 16' decided as the maximum caliber at the Washington Arms Limitation Treaty.
** Given for Type 91 AP (boat-tail) projectiles. When firing the Type 88 AP projectile with a weight of 1,000 kg the chamber length was 2.4319 m, the volume 480.25 liters.
*** The muzzle velocity depended on the weight of shell. The lower velocity was for the heavier projectiles, the higher for the lighter ones. The muzzle velocity changed considerably towards the end of the life.
+ AP = armor piercing; TP = target practice shell; CS = common shell; IC = incendiary shell.
++ Three types of charges were used, namely full (4/4), reduced (3/4), and weak (2/4). There was also a strong charge (full + up to 20%) but used only for trial purposes. 219 kg are given in Shōwa Zōsen-shi, vol. 1, p. 701, and Umi to Sora, 6/1958, p. 51.
+++ Calculated by equivalent full charges the (IJN did not use this term), i.e. strong charge was calculated as two shells fired, reduced charge as ½ shell fired and weak as 1/16 shell fired.

According to the late Rear Admiral Takasu Kōichi, a total of thirty-eight guns were produced in the Weapon Division of Kure Arsenal. The Technical (weapon production) Vice Admiral Noda Tsuruo noted that the Steel Production Division of Kure Arsenal made the ingots for fifty-eight 1A, fifty 2A, and fifty-one 4A tubes for 40 cm guns up to 1921. Horikawa Kazuo and Ondo Shinsaku, in their *Notes on the History of the Former Military Steel Technology*, refer to the examination of seventy-seven 2A tubes (from the first to the final test stages) between 1919 and 1922, which ended with the passing of twenty-three tubes (only 32 percent!), and this result proves the considerable difficulties experienced in the production of these tubes of more than 17 m in length (including test edges).

The principal ballistic data of the 40 cm gun are shown in table 11.

Main Gun Mountings

The mountings were basically copies of the British-built turrets for the Kongō class. The principal improvements introduced by Japanese designers were (1) greater elevation, (2) free loading angles, (3) improved flash tightness in gunhouse and working chamber,[2] and (4) safer loading cages for the upper hoists.

Table 12 summarizes some essential data.

Table 11: Principal Ballistic Data of the 40 cm Gun

Elevation/Range	Angle of fall	Striking velocity	Penetration (AP shell) in mm	
			Vertical (VC)	Horizontal (NVC)
			15,000 m = 406/551 // 826	/165 // 148
20,000 m	21°40'		20,000 m = 272/424 // 429	/190 // 156
20° = 24,100 m	30°26'	420 m/s	24,100 m = 211/287 // 369	/203 // 173
25° = 27,400 m	37°59'	420 m/s		
30° = 30,300 m	44°38'	434 m/s	/234 // 307	/259 // 218
35,000 m			// 273	// 295

Sources:
Fukuda, op. cit., 159; data after the oblique stroke *Umi to Sora*, 5/1958, 78, data after the double oblique stroke and for range 35,000 m (after increasing the elevation angle to 43°) are from Fukuda, op. cit., 88, using Type 91 AP projectile against uniform armor.

Notes:
(1) VC = Vickers Cemented.
(2) NVC = New Vickers Cemented.
Flight time of the projectile for 30,000 m is given as 59 seconds when fired with a muzzle velocity of 780 m/s (*Umi to Sora*, 6/1958, 51).

Table 12: Principal Particulars of the Gun Mounting

Character	40 cm twin mount derived from British Vickers Co. Ltd. type completed in about 1910. Turret structure with strongly armored gunhouse (front shield 305 mm/457 mm VC; sides 230 mm/280 mm; aft 190 mm/190 mm; roof 152 mm – 127 mm/250 mm – 228 mm NVNC; floor 102 mm/102 mm = as completed/after increasing the protection) housing two 410 mm guns in slides and independent cradles with 2.49 m distance between centrelines of barrels. Revolving part of 972 tons weight (after increasing the protection up to 1,124 tons)* with cast turntable training on roller path with equally spaced rollers (except part where roller holders are jointed) of 8.992 m diameter inside a barbette formed of 305 mm VC armor and diameter of 10.210 m
Operation	Hydraulic motor (pump) etc.
Maximum elevation/depression	−5° to +30° (−5° to +43° after modernization conversion)
Elevation/depression speed	8°5'/s
Training motor	Hydraulic pump 150 hp (after modernization hydraulic pump 220 hp)
Training speed	1.58° –3°/s (3°/s are supposed after modernization conversion)
Elevation gear	Hydraulic telescopic tubes (cylinders)
Training gear	Cylindrical worm and worm wheel
Hoists	Two sets per turret of typical British type. Lower hoist: Ammunition hoist cage through central trunk actuated by hydraulic power raises complete round (projectile and powder bags) from handling room to working room (chamber). Upper Hoist: Gun-loading hoist cage brings ammunition to breech from working chamber and is also actuated by hydraulic power
Rate of supply	1.5 rounds/min. (round means projectile and four powder bags), later improved to 2 rounds/min. by the reduction of reloading time
Fuse setting	Manually, usually made on waiting tray in the working chamber
Loading angle	Free (at any angle) loading. Report O-47 (N)-1 states that "the guns are never loaded at elevations above 20° and the breech cannot be opened above 25°." This can partly be confirmed by data in *Umi to Sora*, 5/1958, 76, giving a loading angle of − 5° to +25° before and −3° to +20° after the modernization conversion. The blocking of the breech block is not mentioned but might be correct
Rammer	Power operated chain; one stroke for projectile followed by another one for the four one-quarter powder bags (at first two strokes were necessary to load the powder bags, but it was soon modified to be made by one stroke in order to reduce the loading time by 1.5 seconds)
Fire control system	Director firing but initially no computer. Aiming telescopes/periscopes in the gun house (hoods on the roof). Rangefinder (*Ha shiki* – American Bausch & Lomb type) of 6 m base length mounted on all four turrets.* If the central fire control failed individual aiming and firing of the turrets could be performed. In this case both operations described below were made independently by the gun crew. Later a complete fire control system was fitted
Gun laying	Follow the pointer, i.e., total training (TT) and total elevation (TE) are transmitted from director and shown on receivers (while pointers) in the turrets whose following (red) pointers have to be adjusted with the white ones
Safety arrangement for firing	Only the guns laid correctly, i.e., whose pointers coincide, can be fired.
Rate of fire	1.5–2 rounds per minute. Loading cycle was initially 24 seconds when the guns were laid horizontal (29 seconds when elevated to 30°) but reduced to 21.5 seconds (26.5 seconds) because of the one-stroke loading of the powder bags). Therefore, two rounds/min were theoretically possible but due to the rate of supply the firing of two rounds per minute could not be kept in salvo firing for more than about 15 minutes.
Gun crew	?; 15 in the gunhouse
Manufacturer	Gunnery Divisions of Kure Naval Arsenal and Yokosuka Naval Arsenal
Problems	Wearing of tooth face of worm wheel of training gear; corrosion of interior of elevating cylinder (telescopic tube), difficult handling of work valve for training
Requirements	None in the 1910s till the 1930s but later referring to AA firing as mentioned in a footnote

Note:
* This type was ordered because import from Britain became difficult in World War I. However, this product often had disorders and the accuracy of measurement was inferior compared with the *Bu* (Barr & Stroud) type. Therefore, all rangefinders were replaced by Type 3 10 m double rangefinders (mounted on the superimposed No. 2 and No. 3 turrets) during the modernization conversion.

Two types of turrets were built. The first one was for the Nagato class, with an elevation of 30 degrees, and the second type, designed for the Kaga class, permitted an elevation of 35 degrees. The weight of the *Nagato* turret was 892 tons.

Eighteen turrets (among them, six for the Nagato class) and four turrets (among them, two for the Nagato class) were produced in the Weapon Divisions of Kure Arsenal and Yokosuka Arsenal, respectively.[3] Fourteen turrets (gunhouses) were produced for the Kaga class, but of these, six were transferred to the IJA for coast defense batteries. The remaining eight turrets were refitted to an elevation of 43 degrees, and they replaced the former turrets of *Nagato* and *Mutsu* when the modernization conversion was executed.

Table 13: Principal Technical Data of the 14 cm Secondary Guns	
Designation	50 Cal. 3 Year Type 14 cm Gun
Caliber (mm)	140.0
Weight (metric tons)	5.45–5.92
Total length (m)	7.235
Barrel length (m) (caliber length)	6.999 (50.0)
Shell weight (kg)	38.00
Propellant charge (kg)	10.22
Charge weight (kg)	2.010 (capped common shell modification 2)
Muzzle velocity (m/s)	850
Range (m)	19,750 (elevation 35°)

Source:
Tsutsumi Akio, *Sekai no Kansen*, 854, 110.

Notes:
During the Pacific War the ammunition for these guns included: Capped Common Shell Modification 2 (*Hibō Tsūjōdan Kai 2*), No. 2 Common Shell (*2 Gō Tsūjōdan*), Type 0 Common Shell (*0 Shiki Tsūjōdan*) and the Illumating Shell B (*Shōmeidan Otsu*). It remains uncertain if *Nagato* was equipped with the 14 cm antisubmarine shell (*14 cm Hō Taisendan*) and the Type 3 Illuminating Shell (*3 Shiki Shōmeidan*). Both of which were adopted in 1944.

Table 14: Principal Ballistic Data of the 14 cm Gun		
Elevation/Range	Angle of fall	Striking velocity
20° = 15,800 m	36°30'	320 m/s
25° = 17,500 m	43°40'	328 m/s
30° = 19,100 m	50°25'	347 m/s

Source:
Fukuda, op. cit., 159.

Table 15: Armament of Nagato Before and After Modernization Conversion

	As built	As modernized
Main guns	8 – 40 cm L/45 3 Year Type (4 × 2)	8 – 40 cm L/45 3 Year Type (4 × 2)
Secondary guns	20 – 14 cm L/50 3 Year Type (20 × 1)	18 – 14 cm L/50 3 Year Type (18 × 1)
Small caliber guns	8 – 8 cm L/20 Type 41 (8 × 1)	8 – 8 cm L/20 Type 41 (8 × 1)
Machine guns	3 – 6.5 mm 3 Year Type (3 × 1)	3 – 7.7 mm Lewis Type (3 × 1)
High-angle guns	4 – 8 cm L/40 3 Year Type (4 × 1)	8 – 12.7 cm L/40 Type 89 (4 × 2)
Antiaircraft machine guns	–	4 – 40 mm L/40 Vickers Type (2 × 2)
Torpedo tubes	8 – 53 cm Armstrong Type (4 above, 4 below)	–
Aircraft	–	3 – Nakajima E4N2 floatplanes
Catapults	–	1 – Kure Type No. 2 Model 5 Modification 1
Searchlights	10 – 110 cm	8 – 110 cm
Boats	12 2 – 56' vedette boats 2 – 42' launches 2 – 40' launches 4 – 30' cutters 1 – 30' sampan 1 – 20' sampan	12 2 – 17 m vedette boats 1 – 40' steam launch 2 – 40' launches 4 – 30' cutters 2 – 30' sampans 1 – 20' sampan

Notes:
– Actual bores: 40 cm = 41 cm, 8 cm = 7.62 cm, 53 cm = 53.3 cm.
– The 8 cm L/20 guns were used as saluting guns.
– The 40 mm machine guns were removed in 1939 and instead 20 25 mm L/60 Type 96 (10 × 2) machine guns were fitted.
– The antiaircraft armament was significantly increased during the Pacific War and at Leyte Gulf in October 1944 *Nagato* had eight 12.7 cm high-angle guns and 92 25 mm machine guns (14 × 3 + 10 × 2 + 30 × 1). In 1945 two twin 12.7 cm high-angle guns abreast the funnel were added and in the summer of 1945 *Nagato*'s antiaircraft outfit consisted of twelve 12.7 cm (6 ×) and 52 25 mm (10 × 3 + 5 × 2 + 12 × 1).
– In 1938 three Nakajima E8N1 Type 95 floatplanes were embarked and during the Pacific War Nakajima F1M2 Type 0 floatplanes were also embarked.
– A Kure Type No. 2 Model 3 Modification 2 (*Kure Shiki 2 Gō 3 Gata Kai 2*) catapult had been fitted already in 1933.
– A Type 21 (air search) radar was added in May 1943 and after the Marianas Sea Battle two sets each of radar Type 13 (air search) and 22 (surface search) were added in late June 1944.

Nagato during gunnery trials probably on November 24, 1920, at Iyo-nada, Western Inland Sea, on a photo taken by Kure Arsenal. After speed trials, gun and torpedo trials were conducted the day before the handover. The installation of the 10 m rangefinder on the foremast was not yet completed, indicating the urgency to deliver the ship.

A scene of torpedo trials conducted on March 4, 1922. A rare photo showing the launch of a torpedo from *Mutsu*, probably outside Tokyo Bay. The Nagato class was equipped with four 53 cm surface torpedo tubes and four submerged torpedo tubes. The photograph shows the launch of a 6-Year Type Torpedo (*6 Nen Shiki Gyorai*) from one of the two surface torpedo tubes on the port side. The surface torpedo tubes were located on both sides of the aft funnel, with each side having two torpedo rooms. Each room had one torpedo tube, which could rotate in a limited arc on three circular rails, pivoting near the ship's side (the submerged torpedo tubes were fixed). The 6-Year Type Torpedo, standardized on October 8, 1917, was the first domestically developed wet-heater torpedo. *Sekai no Kansen*

Scene from *Mutsu*'s main gun trials conducted on March 11, 1922, outside Tokyo Bay, showing the third main gun turret, which has been trained to port, firing its two guns. The main guns of this ship were 45-Caliber 3-Year Type 41 cm Guns (*45 Kōkei 3 Nen Shiki 41 senchi Hō*), housed in four twin turrets arranged in a super-firing configuration with two turrets each forward and aft. These guns were first adopted for the *Nagato* and were standardized on July 17, 1917. However, during these trials and on the twenty-ninth of that month, the official designation was changed to 45-Caliber 3-Year Type 40 cm Guns. This was likely done to conceal the fact that the caliber was 0.4 cm larger than the 40.6 cm guns of other countries. The elevation range was –5 degrees to +30 degrees, with a maximum range of 32,500 m. The turret power was hydraulic, and the loading time for shells and propellant was twenty-four seconds. *Sekai no Kansen*

ARMAMENT 53

Nagato during battle training (*sentō kunren*). Although the exact date of the photograph is unclear, it is believed to have been taken around 1924, due to the presence of a cap on the forward funnel. At this time, *Nagato* was incorporated into the 1st Fleet, 1st Squadron (*Dai 1 Kantai, Dai 1 Sentai*). The photograph shows the ship cruising at a high speed of 25 knots, with the 40 cm gun turret trained forward to starboard. Each turret has one gun elevated and one in the loading position, ready for alternate firing. The ammunition capacity was 90 rounds per gun in peacetime and 110 rounds per gun in wartime. *The Maru Special*

Nagato's broadside during target practice using the old battleship *Aki*. The weather was bad and the photo unclear. Although the shots were slightly over, one round landed close, and the target was brilliantly bracketed. *Aki* was being towed at 8 knots, creating a scene that truly evokes actual combat conditions. *Aki* had been completed as a target ship on August 26, 1923, and went down on September 6, 1924, at 17:40 outside Tokyo Bay off Nojima-zaki, after being hit by shells from *Nagato* and *Mutsu*. *The Maru Special*

Nagato with a Heinkel-type launching device (slipway) in May–June 1925, at Yokosuka. Before the introduction of catapults on board, planes could be launched by using a ramp. From late spring to early summer of 1925, Ernst Heinkel was in Japan with a test pilot, and a special ramp was placed on the second turret of the *Nagato* for experiments off the coast of Tateyama. The photograph shows the *Nagato* carrying a Heinkel reconnaissance seaplane (later Type 2 Reconnaissance Seaplane [*2 Shiki Suitei*]). A temporary derrick can be seen to starboard of the foremast.

Another view of the takeoff ramp aboard *Nagato* in the summer of 1925. When the trials had been completed, the device was immediately removed and used on the cruisers *Kako* and *Furutaka*, which were completed the following year.

The forecastle of *Mutsu* around 1930. On the two main gun turrets, there are *Bu*-type (Barr & Stroud) 8 m rangefinders, with the gunnery commander's observation platform located near the center. The turret roof armor is 150 mm thick. The no. 1 gun turret is equipped with an 8 cm practice gun, and the various devices on the turret roof are for aiming practice purposes. *The Maru Special*

The 1st Squadron (*Dai 1 Sentai*) during battle practice (*sentō shageki*) in 1927. *From the left*: Nagato (flagship), *Mutsu*, *Ise*, and *Hyūga*.

Foremast and main gun turrets of *Mutsu* on October 18–22, 1930. This scene depicts the installation of protective equipment such as mantlets (*mantoretto*) on the foremast. The 41 cm L/45-caliber twin gun turrets and the 10 m rangefinder on the upper part of the mast are clearly visible. This photo was taken when *Mutsu* was flagship of the "Blue Fleet" (Vice Admiral Yamamoto Eisuke) during the special grand maneuvers (*tokubetsu daienshū*). *Sekai no Kansen*

Nagato off the coast of Osaka in 1931. The signal yard of the foremast extends straight out to the side, while *Mutsu*'s was angled slightly backward. At that time, *Nagato*'s antiaircraft armament included 7.6 cm high-angle guns, and she also carried reconnaissance seaplanes, but they were launched from the water as she did not have a catapult. However, in 1933 the antiaircraft armament was updated with 12.7 cm high-angle guns and twin 40 mm machine guns. Additionally, she was also equipped with one Kure Type No. 2 Model 3 Modification 2 catapult (weighing 3.3 tons). The standard number of onboard aircraft was three. *Sekai no Kansen*

Mutsu in 1933 with 10 m *Bu*-type rangefinders on gun turrets 2 and 3 and 12.7 cm high-angle guns with associated fire control equipment. Note the searchlight platform between the funnels and the catapult forward of turret 3.

Nagato during gunnery training off Sukumo Bay on May 21, 1936. *Nagato* is steaming at full speed of 25 knots and is firing at a target on her port bow. Until the emergence of *Yamato* and *Musashi*, the 40 cm guns were the trump card of the Japanese fleet. During the reconstruction, the magazines and the shell hoists were modified for type 91 AP shells, and the number of rounds per gun in wartime increased to 130.

Main gun turrets of *Mutsu* after the reconstruction. The forward turrets, the no. 1 and no. 2 main gun turrets, were refitted with guns originally produced for the unfinished battleships *Kaga* and *Tosa*, which had been scrapped due to the Washington Naval Treaty. The guns are ready for alternate firing (*kōgo shageki*), but during the reconstruction, the recoil mechanisms were converted from hydraulic to pneumatic, allowing for continuous salvos (*renzoku seisha*) from all turrets. On the roof are gunfire mirrors (*hōkakyō*), aiming-practice device (*shōjun-enshūki*), covers, and observation windows (*kansoku mado*). The Maru Special

Nagato anchored in Sukumo Bay in May 1937. The second turret is trained to starboard aft and the third turret to the port forward, clearly showing the shape of the 10 m rangefinders installed at the rear of the turrets. During the reconstruction the ship underwent modifications to increase the elevation (from 20 degrees to 35 degrees) of the 14 cm secondary guns. Additionally, the foremost secondary guns on both sides (no. 7 and no. 8) were removed because they often became unusable in rough seas. The photo clearly shows the removed gunport area.

After completing a torpedo attack, a Type 96 Land-Based Attack Aircraft Model 23 (*96 Shiki Rikkō 23 Gata*) flies over the battleship *Nagato* in October 1941. At that time, the mission of the air units, such as the Genzan Air Group (*Genzan Kōkūtai*), was to attack enemy capital ships prior to the fleet's decisive battle and reduce their strength. Torpedo attacks by medium twin-engine attack aircraft with long operational ranges were considered a highly effective tactic, and extensive battleship attack training was conducted at sea. Simultaneously, the surface ships being attacked also carried out antiaircraft combat and evasion training, with both the aviation and surface units striving to improve their skills through mutual effort. At this time, it appears that *Nagato* was in the midst of gunnery training, directing its main guns slightly forward to the port side and taking a position for alternate firing (*kōgo uchikata*). Bunrin-Do

This is probably a scene from a gunnery training (*hōsen kunren*), showing *Nagato*'s forecastle deck and the forward main gun turrets. *Nagato* is steaming at high speed, and the rough sea conditions cause water to crash over the deck. Despite the extensive refit, which included a modification of the bow, seaworthiness was still insufficient. Details such as the nonslip surface on the top of the no. 1 turret and the unique antenna support mast erected on top of the no. 2 turret can be clearly seen. Sekai no Kansen

View of *Nagato*'s aft main gun turrets: the impressive third and fourth 41 cm, 45-caliber twin turrets in October 1941. The 41 cm guns on the Nagato-class battleships had a maximum elevation of 30 degrees and a maximum range of 32,500 m as built. However, after the reconstruction the main turrets were replaced, allowing a maximum elevation of 43 degrees and increasing the maximum range to 38,300 m. Along with the improvements in fire control systems, it can be said that the ship's gunnery capabilities were significantly enhanced. Attention should also be paid to the mushroom-shaped ventilators on the aft deck and the crosstrees on the mainmast.

Battle practice training (*sentō shageki kunren*) of the 1st Squadron in October 1941. A scene viewed from the deck of the *Nagato* toward *Mutsu*. *Mutsu* is firing all main guns at the target. Incidentally, for Japanese battleships before the Nagato class, due to issues with the power mechanisms for gun elevation, training, and recoil, it was difficult to practically use "salvo firing" or "simultaneous firing" (*seihatsu uchikata*) in actual combat. Therefore, the method of firing the left and right guns of each turret alternately, known as "alternate firing" (*issei uchikata*), was used. Simultaneous firing (after 1937 called *issei uchikata*) of all main guns became practically possible only after the reconstruction, which changed the recoil mechanism of the guns from hydraulic to pneumatic and strengthened the hydraulic pumps for turret power. However, from an artillery standpoint, alternate firing (after 1937 called *kōgo uchikata*) continued to be primarily used. Various equipment is attached near the barbette of the third turret, and this photograph, which shows these details, is extremely rare. *Sekai no Kansen*

A 25 mm twin machine gun mount on the foremast of *Nagato*. This particular mount was positioned to port on the lower lookout station (*mihari-sho*). During operation, the gunner (also handling elevation) sat in the left seat, the trainer in the right seat, and the loaders were positioned behind the machine gun. The aiming devices for these machine guns were of the L.P.R. (Le Prieur) type. When *Nagato* and *Mutsu* went to war, they had ten twin 25 mm mounts. The scene was taken in October 1941 in Saiki Bay, and several "Special Type" destroyers are visible in the background. *Sekai no Kansen*

Preparations for the launch of a Type 95 Model 2 Reconnaissance Seaplane (*95 Shiki 2 Gō Suijō Teisatsuki*) from *Nagato* in October 1941. When this photo was taken, *Nagato* had been fitted with a folding catapult Kure Type No. 2 Model 5 Modification 1 (*Kure Shiki 2 Gō 5 Gata Kai 1*), similar to *Mutsu*'s, and a folding derrick. This scene depicts placing the type 95 plane onto the catapult from the trolley on the aircraft transport rails. The standard number of aircraft carried by this type was three, and even at the outbreak of the war, type 95 seaplanes were still aboard. It wasn't until the latter half of 1942 that they were replaced by the new Type 0 Observation Seaplane (*0 Shiki Kansokuki*). Although it is difficult to see, the aircraft numbers written on the vertical tail fins of the onboard aircraft at that time were AI-1 to AI-3, where "A" indicated the 1st Squadron, "I" indicated the flagship, and the number after the hyphen indicated the specific aircraft number.

41 cm type 0 common shells (*0 Shiki tsūjōdan*) aboard *Nagato*, photographed by the US Navy before the nuclear tests at Bikini Atoll. *US Navy*

41 cm type 1 armor-piercing shells (*1 Shiki tekkōdan*) aboard *Nagato*. The change from the type 91 armor-piercing shells (*91 Shiki tekkōdan*) was issued in January 1942, and it was stated that the firing tables for the type 91 should be used. At the Battle of Leyte Gulf, *Nagato* fired forty-five rounds of type 1 armor-piercing shells. *US Navy*

The third (starboard) twin 12.7 cm high-angle gun mounting aboard *Mutsu* in October 1941. The detailed view provides a clear look at the gun's breech and loading mechanism. During a shooting exercise in 1940, using this gun and the Type 91 High-Angle Fire Control System (*91 Shiki Kōsha Sōchi*), the results were recorded as follows: for the basic course (type A), the hit rate was 0.9 percent (at an average firing range of 6,900 m, altitude of 3,200 m, with the ship's speed at 15.5 knots and the target traveling in a straight line at 85 knots). For the applied course (type B), the hit rate was 2.82 percent (at 5,300 m, altitude of 1,500 m, with the ship at 16.6 knots and the target at 84.3 knots). Given these training results, it is evident that hitting US aircraft, which flew at several times these speeds and employed evasive maneuvers, would have been considerably challenging. Due to her loss in 1943, *Mutsu*'s antiaircraft armament was not increased. *Sekai no Kansen*

Fire Control Systems

As the only 40 cm gunned battleships in the IJN, the fire control system of the Nagato class included the most-modern components (except for the high-angle guns), and it may be of interest to quote from Mayuzumi Haruo's *Kanpō Shageki no Rekishi* ("History of naval guns and fire control systems"):[4] "Because *Nagato* was the first capital ship of the IJN armed with 40 cm main guns, it became the model for the following 40 cm gun battleships *Kaga*, *Tosa*, etc. and battle cruisers *Akagi*, *Amagi*, etc. of the Eight-Eight Fleet with regard to fire command weapons, gun battle techniques, improvement of the weapons, and their handling, etc. Every aspect should be considered and investigated from different points of view." Of course, the following enumeration of the instruments can impart only a very rudimentary impression of the complexity of fire directing and the many problems to solve before a gun could be fired.[5]

Table 16: Fire Control Systems		
Item	Before the modernization conversion	After the modernization conversion
Fire directors (*Hōiban*)		
Main guns	One Type 13 fire director each in the main control station atop the foremast and in the auxiliary control station atop the after superstructure. One in the No. 2 main gun turret control station	One Type 94 Model 1 fire director each in the main and auxiliary gun control stations, located at the same positions as earlier. One Type 13 fire director in the forward main gun auxiliary control station. The control station in the No. 2 main gun turret was removed
Secondary guns	One bearing transmitter (*hōkōshijiki*) each in the secondary gun control stations located on both sides of the foremast and after superstructure (it is said that these stations were fitted some years after completion and the fitting of other fire control system components is also uncertain)	One Type 94 fire director for secondary guns fitted in each of the four control stations to divide the fire of the guns on one broadside into two. However, the concentration of both groups of one broadside upon one target was possible and all four groups could be controlled by one director
High-angle guns	No high-angle guns and no fire director until 1932. Jointly with the mounting of 40 cal. Type 89 12.7 cm twin high-angle guns in 1933 a Type 91 high-angle gun fire control system, composed of one Type 91 high-angle fire director and a separate 4.5 m stereo rangefinder was fitted on a platform between the two funnels. One system on each side.	No change of the fire control system but mounted on the antiaircraft control deck newly erected on both sides of the new funnel
Machine guns	No fire control system but usual sights	In 1938 four Type 95 machine gun fire directors for remote control of the newly fitted ten Type 96 25 mm twin machine guns were mounted. One each was mounted on both sides of the foremast and platforms aft of the funnel to control the forward group (six machine gun mounts) and after group (four mounts)
Target-bearing and speed-measuring instruments (*Sokutekiban*)		
Main guns	One Type 13 *Sokutekiban* each on the foremast and after superstructure (?); supposed to have been fitted in 1924/25.	One Type 92 *Sokutekiban* on the foremast; one 12 cm spotting sight on the after superstructure. Some spotting sights distributed on stations on the foremast
Secondary guns	?	Two Type 13 *Sokutekiban* on the foremast

Range measuring – Rangefinders (*Sokkyogi*)		
Main guns	Seven Year type 10 m rangefinder atop the foremast. Four *Ha* (Bausch & Lomb) type 6 m rangefinders on main gun turrets (in case of Mutsu 8 m *Bu* [Barr & Stroud] type).	Type 94 10 m double rangefinder atop the foremast. Two Type 3 10 m rangefinders on turrets No. 2 and No. 3.
Secondary guns	Two *Bu* type 3.5 m rangefinders mounted on the foremast	Four Type 93 3.5 m rangefinders on both sides of the fore and after secondary guns auxiliary control stations. In 1938 these rangefinders were replaced by *Bu* type 4.5 m rangefinders
High-angle guns	Two *Bu* type 2 m high-angle rangefinders, replaced by two *Bu* type 4.5 m stereo high-angle rangefinders in 1933	Replaced by two Type 94 stereo 4.5 m rangefinders fitted on both sides of the antiaircraft control deck
Computers (*Shagekiban*)		
Main guns	Range clock (*Kyori dokei*) Type 10 and successor types in the main gun command station; also range rate panel (*henkyoritsuban*) in the foremast	Type 92 computer in the main gun command station
Secondary guns	Two range clocks Type 10 in the secondary gun command station	Same as before (one each in a separate room to control the fire of each broadside). Said to have been replaced by two Type 94 No. 1 computers in 1939–41
High-angle guns	Two Type 89 computers in the high-angle gun command station	Said to have been replaced by two Type 94 high-angle gun computers Mod. 1
Fire command communication equipment (*Shageki shiki tsūshin sōchi*)		
Main guns, secondary guns, high-angle guns, machine guns	All components of the fire control system were connected by a variety of communication means to transmit data (fire director, target bearing and speed measuring instrument, rangefinders, spotting sights etc.) to the computer, which calculated the firing elements (total training and total elevation) and transmitted them to the guns, and also gave a feedback to other components, prominent among the fire director. The communication means included everything from the primitive (but reliable) voice tube to selsyns and also telephones, high voice telephones etc. As shown on a photo of the main command station of Nagato, showing the partly dismounted Type 92 computer the walls of, the station was full of instruments. When the fire of machine guns was controlled by the machine gun fire director the communication was by selsyn; that is the machine guns followed the movement of the director as long as the electric cable was not severed.	
Searchlights (*Tanshōtō*)		
Main guns, secondary guns, high-angle guns	Ten 110-cm searchlights of which eight were situated on the foremast and two on the mainmast (the two searchlights on the uppermost level of the foremast were termed "direction lights" (*shidōtō*), all others were *shōshatō*). One searchlight command (*shōsha shikisho*) and one auxiliary command (*shōsha yobi shikisho*) station at the foremast	Eight Type 93 110-cm searchlights of which two were still mounted on the foremast (but removed in 1938), while the other six were situated on the searchlight platforms erected on both sides of the funnel. The control stations remained in the foremast and here two Type 92 searchlight controllers were fitted for remote control (same principle as in case of the machine gun fire director)

A front view of *Nagato*'s foremast on a photo from about 1921. Note the 10 m rangefinder mounted high up. The mast consisted of a thick central pillar surrounded by six supporting pillars. At the top is a cylindrical director (*hōiban*).

The impressive "pagoda mast" and forward main gun turrets of *Mutsu* in 1924–26

Nagato acting as the imperial flagship (*Omeshikan*) in July 1925. The details of the foremast are clearly visible, and the names of each part at that time were as follows: from the bottom, the conning tower (*shireitō*; located immediately behind turret 2, housing the wheelhouse [*sōda shitsu*]), the gun group command station (*hōgun shiki-sho*; the section with windows on both sides), the compass bridge (*rashin kankyō*), the lower searchlight station (*kabu tanshō-sho*; also housing the torpedo command station [*gyorai shiki-sho*]), the middle searchlight station (*chūbu tanshō-sho*), the target survey station (*sokuteki-sho*; originally housing searchlights and called the upper searchlight station [*jōbu tanshō-sho*] at the time of construction), the rangefinder station (*sokkyo-sho*; equipped with a 10 m rangefinder [*sokkyogi*]), the top fire command station (*shōrō shiki-sho*; the section with windows), and the main gun fire command station (*shuhō shiki-sho*), and at the top was the main gun firing station (*shuhō shageki-sho*), equipped with a director (*hōiban*). *Sekai no Kansen*

Nagato during battle practice around 1925. Between 1921 and 1926 the average hit rate of *Nagato* and *Mutsu* was only about 3 percent. This was well below the 7 percent for the Kongō class and posed a significant problem for the IJN. One reason for this was the newly adopted multipost foremast, whose vibration significantly affected aiming, observation, and fire control. However, the IJN succeeded in rectifying the problems, and in 1929 the average hit rate reached 13.5 percent at 27,500 m. After this year, the hit rate averaged about 8 percent or more. *Hiraga Archive*

Mutsu's foremast in the late Taishō period, photographed in 1925. This photo clearly shows the details of the foremast, and from the bottom up, it includes the conning tower (*shireitō*), the gun group command station (*hōgun shiki-sho*), the compass bridge (*rashin kankyō*) (equipped with a 3.5 m rangefinder for the secondary guns), the lower searchlight station (*kabu tanshō-sho*), the middle searchlight station (*chūbu tanshō-sho*), the top fire control station (*shōrō shirei-sho*) and searchlight command station (*shōsha shiki-sho*), the rangefinder station (*sokkyo-sho*) (equipped with a 10 m rangefinder), the main gun fire command station (*shuhō shiki-sho*), and the main gun-firing station (*shuhō shageki-sho*). The 10 m rangefinder was mounted on a balcony-style platform with an electric motor that allowed it to rotate on a full-circle rail. In the photograph, this rangefinder is covered with a heat-protection cover. *Sekai no Kansen*

Mutsu's aft main gun turrets and superstructure. This photo is from 1933 and provides a clear view of the aft main gun turrets and the aft superstructure. Noteworthy details include the elevated position of the range clock, compared with its original placement, and the presence of the Type 90 Model 2 Reconnaissance Seaplane (*90 Shiki 2 Gō Suitei*) to starboard. *Sekai no Kansen*

ARMAMENT 69

Nagato photographed from starboard aft sometime between 1926 and 1930. A rare image showing the structure of the rear of the foremast. *Nagato* served as the flagship of the Combined Fleet from December 1, 1925, to December 10, 1928, after which she handed over the flagship role to *Mutsu* for the following two years. Incidentally, the position of the range clock (*renji kurokku*) on the mainmast on *Nagato* and *Mutsu* was slightly different, with *Nagato*'s being set higher than *Mutsu*'s. Note that *Nagato* has 8 m *Bu*-type (Barr & Stroud) rangefinders on all turrets. These had in 1925 replaced the original 6-meter *Ha*-type (Bausch & Lomb) rangefinders.

Image of *Mutsu* probably taken during the special grand maneuvers naval review (*tokubetsu daienshū kankanshiki*) held off Yokohama on August 25, 1933. *Mutsu*, the flagship, underwent significant modifications the previous year. One notable upgrade was the replacement of the 8 m rangefinder on turret No. 2 with a larger 10 m *Bu* type. This replacement was also carried out on turret no. 3. This rangefinder upgrade was probably not carried out on *Nagato*. The photograph clearly shows the substantial covers extending on either side of the turret, indicating the larger rangefinder's presence. This enhancement was part of broader efforts to improve *Mutsu*'s operational capabilities and accuracy in long-range engagements, reflecting the ongoing modernization of the IJN during that period. *Sekai no Kansen*

The foremast of *Nagato* after the reconstruction, pictured in August 1937. During the reconstruction, the foremast was equipped with the latest artillery fire control systems. At the top of the foremast, the type 94 fire control director (*hōiban*) and the type 94 10 m duplex rangefinder were installed. Various devices in the rangefinder station (*sokkyo-sho*) and the main and secondary target survey stations (*sokuteki-sho*) were also renewed. The photo clearly shows the installation status of these various devices. The main guns were also replaced with those manufactured for the unfinished battleship *Kaga*. A 10 m rangefinder is fitted on the second turret.

View from Mutsu's aviation-handling deck (*kōkū sagyō kanpan*), looking up at the aft superstructure, pictured in 1938. This image clearly shows the complex shape of the crosstrees on the mainmast, with the flag of the then commander in chief of the Combined Fleet, Vice Admiral Yoshida Zengo, and the naval ensign (*gunkanki*) at the top. The cylindrical device in the center of the image is the Type 94 Director Aiming Device (*94 Shiki Hōiban Shōjun Sōchi*) (reserve) for the main guns, while the left and right lower parts are the secondary gun (*fukuhō*) directors (*hōiban*) with integrated 4.5 m rangefinders. The section with windows sandwiched between the secondary gun directors is the aft lookout station (*mihari-sho*). Sekai no Kansen

ARMAMENT 71

Sailors receiving instructions from a petty officer on the port side of the main mast aboard *Nagato* in October 1941. This image shows the port side of the aft lookout station on the mainmast. The 4.5 m rangefinder for the secondary guns is visible to the right. *Nagato* has separate installations for the rangefinder and the secondary gun director, whereas *Mutsu* had an integrated setup, making this a distinguishing feature between the two ships. *Sekai no Kansen*

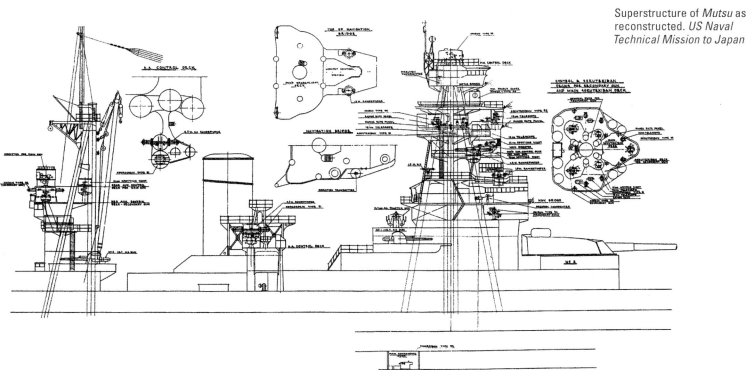

Superstructure of *Mutsu* as reconstructed. *US Naval Technical Mission to Japan*

CHAPTER 10
Protection (Armor and Protective Plating)

The protection system represented a compromise between conventional systems and the "all-or-nothing" system employed for the US Navy battleships from *Nevada* onward. There was a heavy, deep waterline belt that extended from the magazine for no. 1 turret to the magazine for no. 4 turret, but no protection for the ends; the weight thereby saved was invested in horizontal protection over the vitals. In contrast to the US Navy's scheme, however, the middle deck still constituted the main armored deck, and the main deck, which completed the armored "box" of the citadel, had only modest protection.

The following table is provided for sake of convenience and shows only the most-important parts of *Nagato* as completed and after the strengthening.

Item	As completed	After modernization conversion
Waterline belt	305 mm VC (magazines & machinery spaces), 1.98 m above, 0.76 m below waterline. Lower belt 152–76 mm VC (same extent as above), connected to the lower end of the waterline belt and extending 1.53 m below the waterline (data ⁻ waterline are as designed and differ depending upon the displacement)	
Upper belt	229 mm VC, connected to the upper end of the waterline belt and extending upwards to the height of the middle deck where connected to this deck	
Transverse bulkheads	254 mm, fore and after middle deck; 330 mm fore lower deck, 229–76 mm after lower deck (connected to the forward and after ends of the belts). All made of VC except lowermost 76 mm part of after lower deck for which VNC was used	
Longitudinal torpedo bulkhead	Curved 76 mm HT made of three layers of 25.4 mm plates and connected to the lower end of the lower belt and the inner floor of the double bottom	
Bulge	-----	Addition of bulge for maintaining buoyancy due to weight increase and obtaining an expansion room
Middle deck	51 mm HT flat, 76 mm VNC slopes	Addition of 25.4 mm DS
Upper deck	70 mm HT	
Forecastle deck	25 + 25 mm HT	
Magazines	51 mm HT flat (middle deck) 76 mm HT slopes (middle deck) 76 mm HT sides (torpedo bulkhead) 38–25 mm HT floor	Addition of 127 mm NVNC Addition of 279–127 mm NVNC Addition of 64–44 mm NVNC Addition of 38 mm CNC
Main gun houses	305 mm VC front, 40° inclined 229–178 mm VC sides, 30° inclined 190 mm VC rear shield 152–127 mm roof 102 mm VC floor	457 mm VC 280–230 mm VC 228–250 mm VC
Barbettes	305–229 mm VC	Addition of 229–124 mm VC
Casemates	38 mm HT gun shields and 19 mm HT bulkheads between the casemates	
Torpedo tubes on upper deck	Bulkhead between torpedo tubes 25–12.7 mm	----
Conning tower	330–254 mm VC sides, 178 mm VC roof, 76 mm VC floor, 127–76 mm communication tube, 25 mm support	
Steering room	----	51 HT + 51 NC–76 mm VNC roof
	19 mm HT at sides	210 NVNC + 51 mm HT
Funnel uptake	25 mm HT at sides and 19 mm HT at transverses	

Table 17: Protection

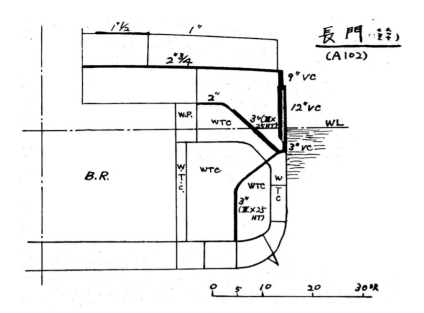

Midship section of the Nagato class as built (design A 102). *Kaigun Zōsen Gijutsu Gaiyō*

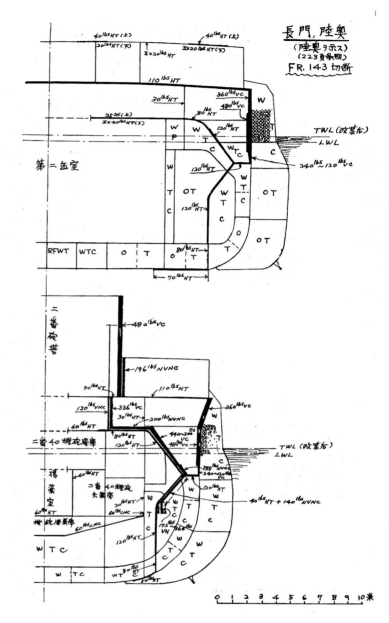

Sections at frames 143 (upper) and 77 (lower) of *Nagato* and *Mutsu* as reconstructed. *Kaigun Zōsen Gijutsu Gaiyō*

The first docking of *Mutsu* after being launched. A photo by Yokosuka Arsenal taken on September 24, 1920, at Yokosuka Arsenal's recently completed Dock No. 5. It was Japan's largest dock at the time, and it was extended in 1923. Considerable work (superstructure and interior) had already been done, and upon docking, the installation of the side armor plates (12" VC armor plates) began in earnest. At the time of construction, the maximum size of armor plates that Japan could produce measured 12" × 20", weighing about 30 tons. In 1920, this was expanded to 15" × 35", of 60 tons. However, this was still smaller than comparative US armor plates. Smaller armor plates meant more joints, resulting in less resistance. At the time of the photo, the ship's weight was 16,854.149 tons, and the number of rivets used was 2,545,406. The number of watertight compartments was approximately 1,000. The distinctive bow shape, common to all combat ships (destroyers and above) of the Eight-Eight Fleet, can be seen.

Photo of *Mutsu* taken in October 1941, just before the outbreak of war, with all main guns trained to port. The modernization work conducted between 1938 and 1939, which included the installation of windscreens and an air defense command station (*bōkū shiki-sho*) on the front of the foremast, can be observed. War preparations included the fitting of watertight steel tubes inside the bulges to ensure buoyancy in the event of damage. Note the degaussing cables fitted on the hull. On *Mutsu* these measures were carried out in June–July 1941.

CHAPTER 11
Complement and Divisional System

Because the IJN had been modeled according to the RN since 1870, customs and daily routine were very similar, so that life aboard in general was not fundamentally different.

Petty officers and ratings lived in each living area on the middle and lower decks, each having a hammock, sea bag, and wardrobe. When enlisted men were berthed and messed in the same compartment, it was equipped with a false wood deck upon which mess tables and mates were placed. The use of bunks for enlisted men was generally nil. Warrant officers had their particular rooms, and officers of ranks more than chief of a division and special-duty officers had private rooms. The use as flagship was realized by fitting official rooms of the flag officer(s) and his staff. The commanding officer also had an official room, his staff the staff officers' room, and other than these, there were officer rooms, gun rooms, etc. These rooms had fine furniture (there were differences according to ranks) and were ventilated and heated[1] like the conning and other important rooms, such as wireless rooms. Lighting was by electric lamps, of which about 2,450 were installed in the ship. Electricity was generated by the generators, as stated before. They were always in operation and supplied the electric power for lighting, ventilation, ice machine, elevator, seawater pumps, coal hoists, etc.

When *Nagato* was designed, ventilation was not considered so important for enlisted men, and air cooling generally was limited to magazines and conning rooms. However, the installations were extended gradually, and crew's living quarters over machinery spaces were included beside officer's quarters, etc.

For ranks above warrant officer, there were four galleys. Those for petty officers and ratings were equipped for cooking for four hundred men each and fitted with every appliance for rice, meat, bread, vegetables, pickles, and fish. Large vats were used to cook rice, since rice could be eaten at every meal. Fish was cooked likewise but could not be eaten freely.

The complement had to make efforts to save water for washing, bathing, and laundry (consumption per twenty-four hours was approximately 170,000 liters) despite the almost 48 tons of pure water distilled per twenty-four hours. Washing and bathing facilities were primitive when compared to European and American standards.

However, as seen from the Japanese point of view, "much attention is paid to sanitation . . . the interior [of the ship] is cleaned daily . . . sanitary rooms [are] always disinfected and inspected by the executive officer, chief surgeon, and chief paymaster. To keep the crew healthy, body inspection is carried out every night, and there are perfectly equipped rooms for medical treatment." In connection, the presence of three medical officers was particularly pointed out.

The complement was divided into twenty-one divisions (*buntai*), and each division was commanded by a divisional officer (*buntaichō*); see table 19.

Table 18: Complement				
Ship/Condition	As built		As reconstructed	
Ship	*Nagato*	*Mutsu*	*Nagato*	*Mutsu*
Source	Directive 164 dated May 31, 1920		Directive 169 dated April 23, 1937	
Officers (*shikan*)	38	38	47	47
Special service officers (*tokumu shikan*)	16	16	16	16
Warrant officers (*junshikan*)	19	19	14	14
Petty officers (*kashikan*)	304	304	328	328
Seamen (*hei*)	954	954	912	910
Total	1,331	1,331	1,317	1,315

Note:
During the Pacific War the complement of both ships increased, and at the time of her loss, *Mutsu*'s complement was about 1,500.

Table 19: Nagato Onboard Organization (December 1943 and After)

Battle organization (Sentō hensei)		Operational organization (Jōmu hensei)	
Department name (Kamei)	Battle station (Sentō haichi)		Division number (Buntai bangō)
Chief gunnery officer (Hōjutsuchō)	Main gun battery (Shuhō hōdai)		1
	Main gun battery (Shuhō hōdai)		2
	Main gun battery (Shuhō hōdai)		3
	Main gun battery (Shuhō hōdai)		4
	Secondary battery (Fukuhō hōdai)		5
	High-angle gun battery (Kōkakuhō hōdai)		6
	Machine gun battery (Kijū hōdai)		7
	Main battery fire control (Shuhō shageki kanbu)		8
	Secondary battery fire control (Fukuhō shageki kanbu)		9
	Measuring division (Sokutekibu)		10
Communications (Tsūshin)	Commuications (Tsūshin)		11
Navigation (Kōkai)	Navigation (Kōkai)		12
Internal affairs (Naimu)	Daily routine (Unyō)		13
	Repair (Kōsaku)		14
	Electricity (Denki)		15
	Auxiliary engine (Hoki)		16
Aviation (Hikō)	Aviation (Hikō)		17
Engine (Kikan)	Engine (Kikai)		18
	Boiler (Kan)		19
Medical affairs (Imu)	Medical affairs (Imu)		20
Paymaster (Shukei)	Paymaster (Shukei)		21

Source:
Nihon Kaigun Nyūmon (*The Imperial Japanese Navy*) (Tokyo: Gakken, 2007), 180.

A view showing visitors aboard the *Nagato* about 1921. As completed, the Nagato class was fitted with improved living spaces and accommodations. This made them among the most-comfortable ships, and they became very popular. The floor space per person in the enlisted personnel's living quarters was 2.6 m^2, significantly improved compared with the 2.2 m^2 aboard the Ise class. Officer quarters, galleys, and bathing facilities were located mostly on the main deck. Additionally, it's worth noting that the Nagato class was the first to introduce Japanese-style (squat) toilets aboard.

Visitors aboard *Nagato* pictured in front of the main gun turrets, with the massive foremast in the background, at Yokosuka in May 1937. It was not uncommon to receive visitors from schools, and Mr. Kageyama Eiichi once told one of the authors that he visited "*Mutsu* or *Nagato* in 1937 or thereabouts and took a guided tour of the ship when it was moored in Yokosuka. . . . It was part of the school excursion, and I was very much impressed with the size, mechanism, guns, and crew's routine work."

COMPLEMENT AND DIVISIONAL SYSTEM

A commemorative photo taken during the emperor's visit to *Nagato*. The photo was taken on the aft deck sometime between November 15, 1938, and August 31, 1939. It is likely from the eight hours from Yokosuka on July 21, 1939. *First row, from the second on the left:* Grand Chamberlain Admiral Hyakutake Saburō; Vice Admiral Katō Takayoshi; Admiral Hyakutake Gengo; Combined Fleet commander in chief Vice Admiral Yoshida Zengo; minister of the Imperial Household, Matsudaira Tsuneo; chief of the naval general staff, Admiral Prince Fushimi Hiroyasu; Lieutenant Colonel Prince Chichibu Yasuhito; His Majesty the Emperor; Lieutenant Commander Prince Takamatsu Nobuhito; one person in between; navy minister, Admiral Yonai Mitsumasa; Vice Admiral Toyoda Soemu; Chamberlain General Baron Nara Takeji; Admiral Hasegawa Kiyoshi; one person in between; and Chamberlain Vice Admiral Hirata Noboru. *Second row, from the ninth on the left:* commanding officer (*Nagato*), Captain Fukutome Shigeru; Combined Fleet chief of staff, Vice Admiral Takahashi Ibō; one person in between; and Rear Admiral Itō Seiichi. *Sekai no Kansen*

Bayonet training (*jūkenjutsu kunren*) beside *Nagato*'s no. 1 turret in October 1941. As part of the crew's training, activities such as bayonet drills, judo, and sumo were conducted on board. Comparing the crew to the 41 cm twin turrets of this class, one can easily see how massive these turrets are. The waterproof cloth (*bōsuifu*) fitted at the base of the main gun barrels is white, but judging from other photos, it seems that after the war began, it was changed to gray on this ship.

The staff members of the Combined Fleet on the compass bridge of the *Nagato* in October 1941. At the time of the outbreak of war, the headquarters (*shireibu*) consisted of 19 staff officers and 103 attached personnel. The staff officers included senior officers, and those responsible for torpedoes (*suirai*), communications (*tsūshin*), navigation (*kōkai*), aviation (*kōkū*), logistics (*senmu*), machinery (*kikan*), and gunnery (*hōjutsu*). In 1944, an operations (*sakusen*) officer was added to this group. The left edge of the image shows the supports of the foremast. *Sekai no Kansen*

Photo of the interior of *Mutsu*'s compass bridge (*rashin kankyō*) taken in October 1941. This is a detailed view from the port side facing the bow, and an unusual glimpse into the layout and equipment within the bridge of a battleship. In the foreground, a low platform serves as the logbook stand (*nisshidai*), while the slightly higher platform ahead of it is the chart table (*kaizudai*). Centrally visible are three pipes, which are voice pipes (*denseikan*) used for communication. Although partially obscured, a magnetic compass (*jikirashin*) is situated beside these pipes. Above the windows, various instruments are fitted, and the deck is covered with wooden gratings to prevent slipping. *Sekai no Kansen*

Crew space (*heiin shitsu*) aboard *Mutsu* in October 1941. Here, petty officers and sailors are seen having a meal. Imperial Japanese naval vessels did not have special dining halls. Sailors had their meals in shared crew spaces like this one and used hammocks for resting. On the right side of the image, the shield of a 14 cm secondary gun is visible. Note that they eat by using chopsticks and that they have separate bowls and plates. *Sekai no Kansen*

CHAPTER 12
Principal Items of the Reconstruction

The modernization of a warship should always be practiced in line with the progress of shipbuilding technology, particularly weapon and engine development, to adapt their offensive and defensive power to the most-recent advances and lengthening their active service life. Another wishful effect was the reduction of the financial burden of the taxpayer. Therefore, naval powers made efforts to maintain the fighting power of their ships by conversions carried out when recognized as necessary by technical progress or for other reasons. Thus, conversions for adaptation were rather frequent. However, the works were mostly rather small scaled and referred to a particular field of technology. After the conclusion of the Washington Treaty, the trend toward major refitting became remarkable and was even intensified when the London Treaty expanded restrictions to other ship classes.

Consequently, and as stated above, the IJN carried out a longtime reconstruction, or modernization conversion (*kindai-ka kaisō*) as the Japanese sometimes called it, of the capital ships in the 1930s. The principal items of the Nagato class may be enumerated as follows:

- Changing of the boilers (the Nagato class did not change the "old" engines and had a speed loss of about 2 knots). This must be criticized as a lack of foresight. Because of the reduction from twenty-one to ten boilers, the forward (bent) funnel was removed.
- Lengthening of the stern by 7.572 m at the waterline in order to reduce hull (propulsion) resistance and also to compensate for the disadvantageous effect of the weight increase. In company with this, the protection of the steering-rudder room, for instance, was increased.
- Increase of the elevation angle of the main guns to 43 degrees from 30 degrees in response to further range increases in the out-range tactic (in company with this and item 6, the gunhouses were replaced by ones produced for the battleships of the Kaga class, as stated earlier).
- Improvement and modernization of the armament other than main guns (secondary guns, high-angle guns, machine guns; for instance, two 14 cm guns on the upper deck were landed, 12.7 cm twin high-angle guns mounted—refer to the tables).
- Removal of the torpedo tubes
- Reconstruction of the multipost mast to a pagoda-type tower mast, and completion of the fire control and command equipment for main and secondary guns, high-angle guns, machine guns, and also night battle facilities, shifting of searchlights, etc.
- Improvement of the horizontal, vertical, and underwater protection
- Fitting of an emergency damage control system (called "emergency flooding and drainage system") in order to maintain/regain stability in case of one-sided flooding (*Nagato* was the first battleship fitted with this system. Before its installation, there was considerable resistance from high-ranking "older" officers who could not believe in the controlled inrush of water).
- Fitting of anti-poison-gas equipment for important rooms and compartments

Nagato after the major reconstruction, in a photo dated February 3, 1936. This image shows the ship departing Kure as the flagship of the Combined Fleet. The ship underwent a major reconstruction at Kure Arsenal from April 1934 to January 1936, and as the photo shows, the appearance changed significantly. The familiar bent funnel was removed, replaced by a single, massive funnel. The reconstruction focused on improving defensive capabilities (enhancing underwater defense with the addition of bulges, strengthening horizontal defense, installing new pumping systems, etc.) and updating offensive power (replacing the main gun turrets to increase elevation and extend the firing range). Additionally, the ship underwent extensive modifications, including replacing the main boilers, revising the bow, lengthening the stern, refreshing the superstructure, and replacing various equipment. The modification of the aircraft equipment and antiaircraft machine guns, as well as increasing the elevation of the secondary guns, was scheduled for later. As a result of this reconstruction, the standard displacement increased by about 20 percent from the original, reaching 39,130 tons.

This photograph, taken on February 20, 1936, documents *Mutsu*'s extensive reconstruction work at Yokosuka Arsenal. At this stage, the hull construction progress was 77 percent, with a total of 6,765.357 tons loaded. The riveting count reached 563,102. The image shows the process of loading the gun barrels for the second turret, highlighting the meticulous efforts to modernize and increase the battleship's firepower and overall capabilities. This reconstruction was part of a broader initiative to update the IJN's fleet during the interwar period.

Mutsu being painted in the spring of 1936. During the reconstruction, the original propellers were replaced by larger three-bladed ones of a diameter of 4.30 m, weighing 10.3 tons each, to match the increased displacement and dimensions. The shape of the blades remained the same—ogival.

PRINCIPAL ITEMS OF THE RECONSTRUCTION

Mutsu during reconstruction, in a photo from May 20, 1936, at Yokosuka Arsenal's Koumi Quay. The image shows the ship moored on the opposite side of the quay, closer to the outfitting workshop. The naval ensign has been hoisted, and crew members can be seen aboard. At this point, the hull construction progress was 88 percent, with a total loaded weight of 7,539.806 tons. The riveting count had reached 598,627. Notably, the 200-ton crane visible in the photo dates to the construction of the battleship *Kawachi*.

On June 20, 1936, at the Yokosuka Arsenal's Koumi Quay, this photograph captures the battleship *Mutsu* nearing the end of her reconstruction. At this stage, the hull construction progress was 91 percent, with a total loaded weight of 7,692.409 tons, and the riveting count had reached 599,166. The ship was just days away from trial runs, indicated by the operational boilers and smoke emitting from the funnel. Key modifications and refits at this stage included reinforcement of the gun turret shields and roofs, upgrades to the turret rangefinders, changes to the bridge and foremast, an increase in the elevation angle of secondary guns and removal of the forward guns, and installation of bulges for improved stability. Notably, many of the weapons for the foremast were still uninstalled, and manhole covers on the bulges remained open.

On July 27, 1936, between 13:00 and 14:00, the *Mutsu* conducted a full-power trial off Tateyama, as part of her postreconstruction sea trials. The day was clear and the sea calm, allowing for a serene and controlled testing environment. During this trial, *Mutsu* had a displacement of 43,496 tons, developed 82,578 shp, and achieved a speed of 25.28 knots. The ship progressively increased speed from various stages of trial runs to full power (10/10), and further tests, such as maneuverability trials, were conducted in the southwestern waters of Tokyo Bay (off Uraga Channel). It can be mentioned that nine naval architecture students from the University of Tokyo and Kyūshū University were aboard during these trials, and one student was the future naval historian Fukui Shizuo. Fukui was positioned in the foremast, and during this trial, the powerful binoculars allowed clear visibility, down to the colors of the swimsuits, of people bathing on the beaches of Hota and Katsuyama. This vivid detail underscores the advanced optical equipment aboard the *Mutsu*, providing critical observational capabilities during naval operations.

On August 20, 1936, *Mutsu* was docked in Yokosuka Arsenal's Dock No. 5 in preparation for the final sea trials. The reconstruction was nearly completed, with the ship having a loaded weight of 7,989.671 tons, and a total of 602,344 rivets used. At this stage, the hull had been fully painted and repair work was finished, and the dock was partially filled with water. The ship was awaiting final adjustments to the compass and other navigational equipment before leaving the dock.

In January 1937, *Mutsu* was photographed anchored at Yokosuka off Azumasaki. Having completed the major reconstruction, *Mutsu* returned to the fleet but underwent additional modifications to the aviation equipment from December 1936, and this photo shows the modifications made. The aviation deck (*kōkū kanpan*) at the aft section was lowered by one deck. The catapult was replaced with the Kure Type No. 2 Model 5 (*Kure Shiki 2 Gō 5 Gata*) catapult, and a new derrick was installed for handling aircraft. The newly installed 4-ton folding derrick is prominently visible in the photo, reflecting the ship's updated capabilities in launching and retrieving reconnaissance aircraft, which were essential for naval operations at the time. *The Maru Special*

PRINCIPAL ITEMS OF THE RECONSTRUCTION

Mutsu immediately after the extensive reconstruction at Yokosuka on January 30, 1937. The reconstruction significantly increased *Mutsu*'s fighting power, extending the maximum range of the main guns to 38,300 m. In addition, substantial improvements were made to the ship's armor protection. The magazine armor was reinforced to withstand hits from the ship's own type 91 armor-piercing shells (*91 Shiki tekkōdan*) at ranges between 20,000 and 28,000 m. Similarly, the armor protection for the main gun turrets and other critical areas was also considerably strengthened. The engine room was reinforced to endure hits from 36 cm shells at comparable distances, providing enhanced survivability. A notable change visible in the photograph is the updated position of the catapult, which was revised just after the major reconstruction in late 1936 to early 1937, similar to changes made on the *Nagato* in 1937. However, the replacement of the catapult itself, from the Kure Type No. 2 Model 3 Modification 2 (*Kure Shiki 2 Gō 3 Gata Kai 2*) to the Kure Type No. 2 Model 5 Modification 2 (*Kure Shiki 2 Gō 5 Gata Kai 1*), was carried out separately within the same year.

The reconstructed *Mutsu* off Azumasaki, Yokosuka, on *February 3–4, 1937*. On the afternoon of February 3, the ship is shown hurrying to prepare for the prewar training, welcoming Vice Admiral Yonai Mitsumasa, commander in chief of the Combined Fleet. In the background, a Type 95 Reconnaissance Seaplane (*95 Shiki Suitei*) is being loaded.

Mutsu sometime between March 8 and 13, 1937. This angle shows that there is no machine gun platform behind the funnel. During the reconstruction, the 40 mm Vickers machine guns remained, but in 1939, ten 25 mm twin machine guns and Type 95 Machine Gun Directors (*95 Shiki Kijū Shiki Sōchi*) were installed, and a machine gun platform was added behind the funnel. The 14 cm single-mounted guns visible on the sides of the ship had their range extended during the reconstruction, achieving a maximum range of 19,750 m (at a maximum elevation of 35 degrees). Incidentally, these secondary guns used hydraulic power for training, but elevation was done manually, which required considerable physical strength. *Sekai no Kansen*

Mutsu at Sasebo sometime between March 8 and 13, 1937. A ship's steamboat is moored to the portside lower boom. From January 21, 1937, to December 15, 1938, this ship served as the flagship of the Combined Fleet (Admiral Nagano Osami), and the flag can be seen at the top of the mainmast.

A view from the upper part of the *Mutsu*'s foremast looking aft in 1938. Note the lattice for rainwater cover (*amimizuōi*) and the baffle plates at the top of the funnel, as well as the shape of the aft superstructure when viewed from the direction of the bow. The aft tripod mast is very thick, and its upper part is painted black, similar to the top of the funnel (in the IJN painting it was referred to as *toshō*). Pay attention to the aerial wires for communication, which are stretched vertically and horizontally. *Sekai no Kansen*

Nagato photographed in the fall of 1937 at Sasebo. The ship's appearance after the reconstruction is well shown. The shape of the bow was changed to improve seaworthiness and became similar to that of *Mutsu*'s. The large 2.8 m wide bulges attached to the sides of the ship are also clearly visible. The structure of the bulges was the same as that on the Ise-class battleships, with a combination of riveted and welded construction, outer plates of 8–12 mm, oil tanks and two watertight compartments, and an approximate flooding capacity of 45 tons per compartment. The upper parts were planned to be filled with watertight steel pipes as a countermeasure against damage, but these were not fitted at this time. To prevent a decrease in speed, the stern was lengthened, and the stern walk was abolished.

This photograph, taken from the anchor deck (*ikari kanpan*) of *Mutsu*, looks up at main gun turrets no. 1 and no. 2 and the foremast in October 1941. Note that the turret rangefinder on the no. 2 turret has been replaced with a 10 m rangefinder during the reconstruction.

The foremast and forward gun turret group of *Nagato* in October 1941. At this time, *Nagato* was the flagship of the Combined Fleet, commanded by Admiral Yamamoto Isoroku. Viewed from the side, the arrangement of the support pillars that make up the foremast is clearly visible. Although the appearance and performance of the foremast had changed drastically since its construction, its basic structure remained unchanged. *Sekai no Kansen*

Nagato in October 1941. From this angle the foremast appears to be unduly tall, giving the ship a sense of heaviness. On the aviation-handling deck (*kōkū sagyō kanpan*), port side aft, are parked two Type 95 Reconnaissance Seaplanes. The bulge at the base of the crane used for handling aircraft, fitted in 1937–38, is clearly visible. The crane had a lifting capacity of 4 tons. During the reconstruction, the boilers were replaced, reducing the number of boilers from the original twenty-one to ten (four large, six small) and reducing the boiler room space by over 20 percent. However, the engines received only partial upgrades, resulting in almost unchanged output. While efforts were made to reduce underwater resistance by extending the stern, the increased weight slightly decreased the speed. War preparations in April–June 1941 included the filling of watertight steel pipes into the bulges, and the fitting of degaussing cables. *Sekai no Kansen*

Nagato at Hashirajima in August 1942. On February 12 of the same year, *Nagato* handed over the position as the flagship of the Combined Fleet to the new battleship *Yamato*. Since the start of the war, *Nagato* had remained in home waters, and on May 29 she set out to support the Midway operation. However, the Japanese aircraft carrier task force was decimated, and with nothing to show for it, *Nagato* returned to Hashirajima on June 14. This photo was taken in August, around the time when US forces landed on Guadalcanal Island, but *Nagato* did not participate in the Guadalcanal campaign.

Portside view of *Nagato* in October 1941. This is an imposing appearance taken from the magazine *G. T. Sun* (*Graphic Time Sun*). This photo and others taken during this time are probably from October 19 to 23, when *Nagato* visited Saiki Bay and steamed in Suō Nada. Incidentally, the same company was responsible for taking the navy's archive photos, and during this time they captured images of various ships, including *Nagato*, *Mutsu*, the aircraft carrier *Zuikaku*, the heavy cruiser *Furutaka*, the light cruiser *Abukuma*, the destroyers *Hibiki* and *Yūgiri*, and the submarine *I 69*. The reporting team also saw the battleship *Yamato* in Suō Nada, but unfortunately they were not permitted to take pictures. *Sekai no Kansen*

Nagato's after turrets and mainmast in August 1942. The massive main guns are impressive. These turrets were originally manufactured for the battleships *Kaga* and *Tosa* and were later mounted on this ship with modifications to increase their elevation, reinforce the armor (adding 152 mm to the 305 mm front shield), and improve the loading mechanisms. Compared with the original turrets, the angle of the front shield is different (45 instead of 40 degrees), resulting in a distinct appearance. Additionally, in 1940, 124 mm of armor was added to the barbette sections of the second and third turrets, bringing the total thickness to 429 mm. *Sekai no Kansen*

Front view of *Nagato* in August 1942. The details of the bridge structure, which underwent significant changes during the reconstruction, can be discerned. The names of each part of the bridge structure, from bottom to top, are the conning tower (*shireitō*) (hidden by the second turret), the forward secondary gun reserve command station (*fukuhō zenbu yobi shiki-sho*) (formerly the gun group command station [*hōgun shiki-sho*]), the compass bridge (*rashin kankyō*), the lookout station (*mihari-sho*) (including the lookout command station [*mihari shiki-sho*] and forward searchlight station [*zenbu tanshō-sho*]), the forward main gun reserve command station (*shuhō zenbu yobi shiki-sho*) (the part covered with canvas), the main gun target survey station (*shuhō sokuteki-sho*), the air defense command station (*bōkū shiki-sho*) (equipped with a type 94 10 m), the battle bridge (*sentō kankyō*) (the part with the upper windows), and the top being the main gun-firing station (*shuhō shageki-sho*), equipped with a type 94 director (*hōiban*). By the way, the forward reserve gun control station of *Nagato* had glass windows on both sides, while *Mutsu*'s was covered with canvas. Additionally, the front round windows of this area are two on *Nagato* and four on *Mutsu*.

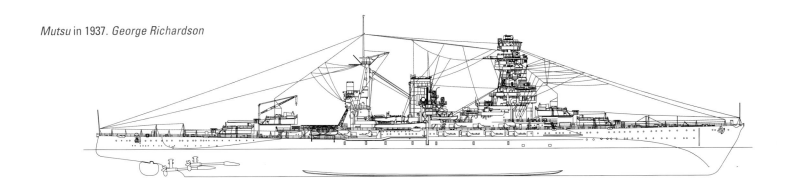
Mutsu in 1937. George Richardson

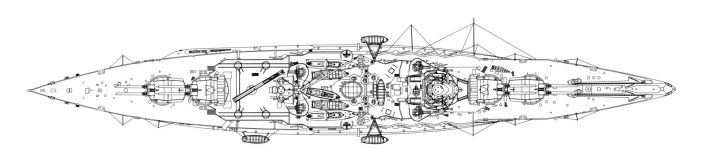

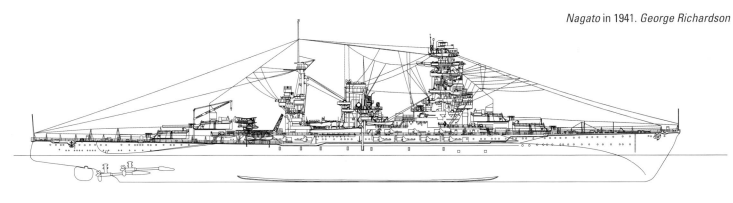
Nagato in 1941. George Richardson

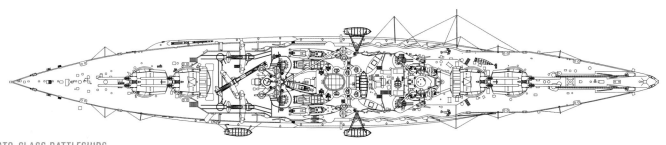

CHAPTER 13
Operational Histories

After commissioning, both ships served as flagships (*Nagato*'s career as flagship was the longest) and division ships and executed peacetime duties such as individual, division, and fleet training; taking part in maneuvers; and visiting ports in Asia for friendship and demonstration (Tsingtao, Amoy, and other Chinese ports, Southern Islands, and also British Hong Kong). *Nagato* became a first reserve ship or training ship of the Naval Gunnery School (to it the strongest capital ship was always allotted), also at the time of *Mutsu*'s modernization conversion. After the beginning of the Sino-Japanese Incident in 1937, some support operations were made, including transportation of army forces.

They were frequently refitted in order to secure their level of fighting power, or when modified weapons and equipment were adopted, or to remove defects and improve their capabilities. In the 1930s the modernization conversion was executed to upgrade their capabilities in response to the modified strategical conception and to satisfy the tacticians.

After the beginning of the Pacific War, the battle fleet was held back at Hashirajima for the "decisive battle," and it was often in standby function in the Inland Sea, later also from the forward base at Truk. The first duty was remote protection of the Pearl Harbor Air Attack Force, and then both ships were part of the main body at the Battle for Midway in June 1942, but they did not engage the US forces because of the 300-mile distance (initially intended to be 600 miles!) to the task force. After a reorganization, support for the forces operating for the recapture of Guadalcanal was provided from the Truk Atoll. *Mutsu* returned to Japan in January 1943 and undertook mainly training duties besides standby functions, before blowing up on June 8, 1943, at Hashirajima, due to a magazine explosion, with heavy loss of life.

Nagato again advanced to Truk in August 1943 to support the operations in the Solomon Islands area and participated in the unsuccessful raid to the Marshall Islands in October 1943. She left Truk on February 1, 1944, for Rabaul because of the imminent danger that this base would be attacked by an enemy task force, but this danger plus a fuel problem forced her to depart Palau for Lingga anchorage in the same month, where she was engaged in training, interrupted by a short stay at Singapore in the first half of April. In May she advanced to Tawi Tawi and took part in the Marianas Sea Battle in June and was back at Lingga anchorage in July after a short stay in the Inland Sea, in preparation for the next operation. She took part in Operation Victory One (*Shō Ichi Gō Sakusen*) in October as a member of the First Raiding Force (Kurita Force), was damaged by two bomb hits and near misses, and fired on enemy ships for the first time on October 25. *Nagato* returned to Japan in November and was used as a guard ship of Yokosuka Naval Station. Moored in the port, she was damaged by US air raids but was the only "operable" Japanese battleship at the end of the war. After the termination of hostilities, she was handed over to the Allied forces and was used as a target at the atomic-bomb experiments at Bikini Atoll, sinking there on July 29, 1946.

This short summary makes evident that the active participation in operations was extremely rare. However, the poor strategic and tactical handling of both ships should not be a discredit to the designers, and it should always be kept in mind that the design was started roughly ten years after the design of capital ships had first begun in Japan. In view of this fact, a fast progress of naval architecture may be noticed.

Mutsu as seen from *Nagato* on October 17, 1924. This photo, taken from *Nagato*, shows the main force (*shuryoku*) of the Combined Fleet (*Rengō Kantai*) in the late Taishō period. In the foreground is *Mutsu*, followed by the Fusō-class battleships and Kongō-class battle cruisers. As can be seen from the photo, the low freeboard of the bow combined with the spoon-shaped bow of this class made it prone to taking on waves when sailing at high speed in rough seas. The spray from the waves affected the rangefinders and other equipment, having an adverse impact on the gunnery. Note the rangefinder on *Nagato*'s turret and the fittings on the aft deck. *Sekai no Kansen*

Nagato at Etajima as the imperial flagship for the crown prince, photographed on July 14, 1925. On the morning of the twelfth, *Nagato* departed Yokosuka with the crown prince (later Emperor Shōwa) aboard to attend the graduation ceremony of the fifty-third class of the Naval Academy (*Kaigun-heigakkō*) and to observe the war games of the Combined Fleet. *Nagato* arrived at Etajima on the morning of the fourteenth. This photo was taken on that occasion, with the ship fully decorated and the crown prince's flag displayed at the top of the mainmast. Attention should also be paid to the details of the stern walk (*sutān wōku*), auxiliary anchor, and fairleader at the stern. After this, the ship proceeded to the war games (*sengi*) held outside Saiki Bay. *Sekai no Kansen*

The Imperial Japanese Navy's special grand maneuvers (*tokubetsu daienshū*) of 1927 were conducted from October 11 to 24, 1927. The second phase of the maneuvers, held from the October 22 to 24, was personally supervised by Emperor Shōwa. The exercise area was off the southern coast of Honshū and to the south, with the main forces of the blue and red fleets engaging in a decisive battle from the twenty-third to the morning of the twenty-fourth in stormy conditions. *Mutsu* served as the imperial ship (*Omeshikan*), departing Yokosuka at 11:30 on the twentieth for the exercise area. The photograph shows *Mutsu* shortly after departing Yokosuka, with the emperor's flag flying on the mainmast. *Sekai no Kansen*

An overhead view of *Nagato* taken in Saiki Bay on July 15, 1925. This photo gives a good view of the full-circle rail with the 10 m rangefinder.

OPERATIONAL HISTORIES

The flagship *Nagato* at the grand maneuvers naval review (*daienshū kankanshiki*) in 1927 off Yokohama, photographed on October 29. This was a navy ministry commemorative photo. Having spent 1925 as a training ship (*renshūkan*), albeit engaged in many special missions, *Nagato* resumed the role as the flagship of the Combined Fleet for three years, starting in 1926. In the fall of 1927, a grand maneuver took place, followed by a fleet review off Yokohama on October 30 (with *Mutsu* as the imperial ship). This photo shows *Nagato* during the rehearsal the day before. The review day was rainy, foggy, and cold, but the rehearsal day had fine weather. In the photo, *Nagato* (the lead ship in the first column) is visible ahead of *Ise*, *Hyūga*, *Yamashiro*, and *Fusō*, with only their masts barely visible. To the left is the imperial ship column, with *Mutsu* immediately to the left of *Nagato*'s bow, followed by the escort ships *Abukuma*, *Yura*, and *Kuma*, from right to left. The far left of the photo shows *Kako* (the third ship in the second column), followed by *Furutaka* (behind *Kuma*), *Aoba*, *Kinugasa*, and *Ōi*, from left to right. On the far right is the first outer column's auxiliary ship (seaplane tender) *Notoro*.

Nagato about 1928. Note the aircraft parked forward of main gun turret 3.

Nagato departing Hong Kong on April 14, 1928. On April 9 of the same year, *Nagato*, along with the 1st Squadron's (*Dai 1 Sentai*) *Mutsu* and *Ise* and the 1st Destroyer Squadron (Dai 1 Suirai Sentai), with the light cruiser *Tenryū* as flagship, made an official visit to Hong Kong. In response, Britain welcomed them with ships from the Eastern Fleet, including the flagship, the cruiser *Hawkins*. The photo was taken by a foreign vessel as *Nagato* was departing Hong Kong.

Mutsu departing Hong Kong on April 14, 1928. On April 9, this ship, in company with *Nagato* and *Fusō*, visited Hong Kong, and this image captures the departure scene. It was uncommon for Japanese battleships to visit foreign ports due to fuel and national defense considerations. While this photo resembles the one of *Nagato*, differences can be noted, such as the canvas-covered gun group command station (*hōgun shiki-sho*) below the compass bridge (*rashin kankyō*). Additionally, among the two anchors visible on the starboard bow, the forward one is the main anchor, and the rear one is the secondary anchor, which was later removed.

Mutsu steaming at slow speed probably between December 1928 and November 1929. From December 1928 to December 1930, *Mutsu* served as the flagship of the Combined Fleet, replacing *Nagato*. The admiral's flag flying from the top of the mainmast is believed to be that of Admiral Taniguchi Naomi, the commander in chief. The aft main gun turrets are also visible. It was said that by using the ship's 41 cm guns, a *Fusō*-class battleship could be incapacitated with twelve to sixteen rounds, depending on the range. A reinforcing truss for the derrick used to handle the floatplanes is installed on the yardarm of the mainmast.

Nagato anchored in Saiki Bay around March 1931. This scene captures a moment during gunnery training (*hō kunren*) at anchor, with the second turret elevated and the third turret trained to port. A truss-like structure can be seen at the base of the crosstrees (*kurosu tsuri*) on the mainmast; this is a reinforcing outrigger for installing a derrick used for handling aircraft. Around 1930, *Nagato* also underwent modifications, including the installation of a funnel rainwater protection (*amamizu yoke*).

The flagship of the Combined Fleet, *Mutsu*, entering Kōbe during fleet training (*kantai kunren*), probably sometime between June 12 and 14, 1930. The 5,500-ton-class light cruisers in the background are *Yura* (*left*) and *Nagara* (*right*). Kure Maritime Museum

Nagato with a bent funnel photographed in early September 1931. This is a splendid image of the ship sailing off Sarushima after departing Yokosuka as the flagship of the Combined Fleet. It shows the appearance after the forward funnel was bent as a measure against smoke exhaust issues. The work to bend the funnel was carried out from the end of 1924 to March 1925. During her lifetime, this "bent-funnel period" was the most glamorous era for the battleship *Nagato*. The phrase "*Mutsu to Nagato wa Nihon no hokori*" (*Mutsu* and *Nagato* are Japan's pride), as recited in prewar cards, refers to this silhouette of the ship.

Mutsu at Sasebo on January 25, 1933, prior to the reconstruction that began the following year. By this time, *Mutsu* had undergone numerous changes since commissioning. From late 1932 to early 1933, searchlight platforms and antiaircraft systems had been installed on both sides of the funnels, and four twin 12.7 cm high-angle guns were added, replacing the older 8 cm high-angle guns. The bridge and foremast also saw several new installations and modifications. Additionally, a catapult was installed between the mainmast and the third turret.

This photograph of *Mutsu*, taken in early to mid-August 1933, during the grand maneuvers of that summer, depicts the flagship of the "Blue Fleet," preparing for combat (*rinsen-junbi*). The maneuvers were deliberately scheduled during the height of the summer heat to study tropical operations in the South Seas region. The image, taken from atop the foremast, shows *Mutsu*'s crew wearing straw tropical hats as they make final combat preparations. The barrels of twin 12.7 cm high-angle guns are visible to the left and right of the image, along with the 110 cm searchlights on either side of the funnels, with shrapnel protection (*danpen bōgyō*) in place.

Nagato at the grand maneuvers naval review (*daienshū kankanshiki*) rehearsal at 12:00 on August 24, 1933. This photograph was taken by Fukui Shizuo from the heavy cruiser *Maya*. During a period of intense international tension, Japan conducted large-scale exercises in the South Seas, culminating in an impressive fleet review. As the flagship of the "Red Fleet's" 4th Fleet, *Nagato* led the main force, which included the modernized battleships *Fusō*, *Kirishima*, and *Ise*. *Nagato* had already been equipped with twin 12.7 cm high-angle guns and the associated gunnery systems. New additions included a searchlight platform between the funnels, a Kure Type No. 2 Model 3 (*Kure Shiki 2 Gō 3 Gata*) catapult, and two twin 40 mm machine guns. From left to right in the distance can be seen the aircraft carrier *Kaga* (flagship of the 1st Carrier Division [*1 Kōsen*]), *Mutsu* (flagship of the "Blue Fleet"), the submarine tender *Jingei* (flagship of the 1st Submarine Division [*1 Sensen*]), and the oiler *Ondo* carrying spectators. The lead ship, *Chōkai*, is barely visible beyond *Nagato*'s No. 4 turret.

Mutsu after maneuvers and preparing for the naval review off Yokohama on August 25, 1933. During this period, *Mutsu* underwent several upgrades, including the replacement of the antiaircraft guns, the installation of 40 mm machine guns, and the addition of a catapult. The rangefinders on the second and third gun turrets were updated to 10 m *Bu*-type models in January 1933. The foremast has also been modified, extending the front of the target survey station (*sokuteki-sho*). The searchlights on the lower section were relocated to a new platform between the funnels, because the position was made into the main gun forward reserve command station (*shuhō zenbu yobi shiki-sho*). The lower lookout station (*mihari-sho*), projecting under the bridge, was a temporary measure; in subsequent major refits, it would be relocated above the compass bridge.

This photograph, taken in August 1933 during the fleet review off Yokohama, captures the moment when *Mutsu* fires a salute using the newly installed twin 12.7 cm high-angle guns. These guns, replacing the older 7.6 cm high-angle guns, were equipped with the Type 91 Antiaircraft Fire Control System (*91 Shiki Kōsha Sōchi*), also installed in 1933. In the left background, the aircraft carrier *Kaga* can be seen. *Sekai no Kansen*

Mutsu off Sumoto, Awaji-shima, not far from Kōbe, during the 4th Fleet's grand maneuver on October 29, 1936. The large ships from the left are the battleship *Hyūga*, the light cruiser *Ōi*, and the light cruiser *Kitakami*.

Nagato anchored in Ariake Bay, photographed between January and April 1937. This image shows the main force of the Combined Fleet, with *Nagato* in the foreground and *Mutsu* beyond. Although the image lacks some clarity, it has some merit. The light cruiser in the left background is a ship of the Nagara class.

A photo of *Mutsu* taken from the foremast of *Nagato* in early 1937. At that time, the order of the 1st Fleet's 1st Squadron was *Mutsu* (flagship), *Nagato*, and *Hyūga*. Admiral Nagano Osami, who was the commander in chief of the Combined Fleet and the 1st Fleet, was aboard *Mutsu*. During a gunnery practice in 1937, *Mutsu*'s firing accuracy was remarkable: at a distance of 20,000 m, the pattern measured 35 m laterally and 220 m in range. *Sekai no Kansen*

Mutsu with units of the 1st and 3rd Squadrons on May 10, 1937. *Mutsu* is closest to the camera, with *Nagato* beyond and *Hyūga* beyond her (all 1st Squadron). To the right is *Kirishima*, with *Haruna* in the distance (both 3rd Squadron).

Nagato at anchor in Kagoshima Bay (Kinkō Bay) in December 1937. After completing her major refit, the ship was incorporated into the 1st Squadron of the 1st Fleet. However, following the outbreak of the Second Shanghai Incident in August 1937, *Nagato* was tasked with transporting army units to Shanghai. Subsequently, in December, *Nagato* was assigned as a training ship. The photo is believed to have been taken when she was used as a training ship. Shortly after, *Nagato* underwent modifications to the aviation equipment, which had not been completed during the major refit. As seen in the photo, the aviation deck, catapults, cranes, and other aviation equipment at the stern are still unchanged.

Mutsu seen anchored in the calm waters of Ariake Bay, Kyūshū, in September 1938. Awnings can be seen on the deck, providing shelter from the sun.

This photograph of *Mutsu* was taken by the Royal Navy (HMS *Birmingham*) on October 21, 1938, at an offshore anchorage at Amoy, China. The image was enlarged from a negative seized by the IJN in the darkroom of the operations room at the former British fleet headquarters in Seletar Naval Base, Singapore, shortly after its occupation in early March 1942. The original negative was sent to the naval general staff.

Photograph of *Nagato* entering Tsingtao in March 1939. This picture was taken when the Combined Fleet cruised in the South China Sea. *Nagato* belonged to the 1st Fleet, 1st Squadron, of the Combined Fleet, serving as the flagship, and formed the squadron with *Ise* and *Fusō*. The light cruiser of the Nagara class visible on the left side of the screen is presumed to be *Yura*, the third ship of the 8th Squadron, 1st Fleet, and the ship to the right is the aircraft carrier *Ryūjō*. About three years have passed since the completion of the reconstruction, and during 1937 to 1938, various improvements were made, including the installation of 25 mm twin machine guns, the renewal of aviation equipment (changing the installation position of the catapult, replacing it with a Kure Type No. 2 Model 5 Modification 1 catapult with a capacity of 4 tons, and refurbishing the aviation-handling deck), increasing the elevation angle of the secondary guns, and installing chemical weapon defense equipment.

Mutsu in Hiroshima Bay around 1940. Note the new machine gun stand behind the funnel, with four twin 25 mm mountings on two levels.

Nagato photographed from *Mutsu* during the grand maneuver in September 1940. *Nagato* had her 25 mm machine guns installed in 1938, and *Mutsu* received her guns in 1939. The 40 mm machine guns were removed.

Mutsu (*left*) and *Nagato* of the 1st Squadron are sailing side by side in October 1941. In the distance is an escorting destroyer. *Bunrin-Do*

Mutsu at sea in 1941. The presence of twin 25 mm machine gun mounts behind the funnel indicates that the photo was taken after 1939. When the reconstruction of the Nagato class was discussed, there were some doubts about converting the original high-speed battleships into medium-speed ones, and some were of the opinion that armor protection should be sacrificed in order to make them comparable to the high-speed Kongō class. However, the rigid adherence to the decisive battle doctrine prevailed.

A photo from the heavy cruiser *Atago* taken on August 23, 1942, off the Solomon Islands. This image captures the Advance Force (*Zenshin Butai*) steaming in port line-of-bearing (*hidarisentō tanteijin*) formation. Positioned on the catapult is a Type 95 Reconnaissance Seaplane (*95 Shiki Suijō Teisatsuki*), ready for immediate launch. The ships, *from front to back*, are the heavy cruisers *Takao*, *Maya*, and *Myōkō*, followed by the light cruiser *Yura*, and, in the distance, the battleship *Mutsu*. Note that part of the 12.7 cm twin high-angle gun barrels on *Atago* is painted white, a tactical measure to ensure visibility of the gun's movement even during nighttime operations. *The Maru Special*

Photo from the evening of August 27, 1942, from the heavy cruiser *Atago*, the flagship of the 2nd Fleet (*Dai 2 Kantai*); this image shows the fleet in starboard line-of-bearing (*migisentō tanteijin*) formation. The ships in formation, from closest to farthest, are the heavy cruisers *Takao* and *Maya*, the battleship *Mutsu*, and the heavy cruisers *Myōkō* and *Haguro*. This photograph captures the fleet just days after the Battle of the Eastern Solomons, when the 2nd Fleet was actively seeking enemy forces in the Solomon Sea area. *The Maru Special*

Photo from the heavy cruiser *Atago* on August 30, 1942. This image captures the 2nd Fleet changing from line-abreast (*ōjin*) to line-ahead (*jūjin*) formation. Following *Atago* are the heavy cruisers *Takao*, *Maya*, *Myōkō*, and *Haguro* and the battleship *Mutsu*. *Atago*'s deck features a Type 0 Reconnaissance Seaplane (*0 Shiki Suitei*), although *Atago* typically carried the Type 95 Reconnaissance Seaplane (*95 Shiki Suitei*) at the time. This suggests that the type 0 (Zero) seaplane might have been temporarily assigned from the seaplane carrier *Chitose*. The distinctive white line on the central part of the mainmast, along with the "ball" and "figure 8" markings on either side, indicates the rudder angle indicator. This device signals the ship's rudder position to the following vessels. During this period, the 2nd Fleet was operating as a support force (*shien butai*) for attacks on Guadalcanal, providing crucial naval presence and reconnaissance capabilities. *The Maru Special*

The Loss of the Mutsu

On June 8, 1943, the ship was anchored at Hashirajima anchorage. At that time, *Nagato*, *Fusō*, the heavy cruiser *Mogami*, and the light cruiser *Ōyodo* were also anchored there. *Mutsu* was scheduled to change its anchorage position starting from 13:00 hours to transfer the flagship buoy to *Nagato*.

Shortly before this operation, *Nagato* arrived and stopped alongside *Mutsu*'s starboard side. Meanwhile, on board *Mutsu*, it was the rest period after lunch. However, shortly after noon, around twelve o'clock, there was a sudden explosion of smoke in the vicinity of the aft turret. A massive explosion occurred. This explosion blew up the huge no. 3 turret of *Mutsu* to about the same height as the bridge, and the hull broke in two near the no. 4 turret, with the bow sinking rapidly. However, the stern remained afloat for about four hours after the explosion, with the stern raised, allowing rescue operations to take place.

Confronted with the immediate catastrophe, *Nagato* immediately suspected a torpedo attack by enemy submarines. Therefore, she quickly moved away from the scene. Once she reached what seemed like a safe distance, she dispatched boats for rescue operations. The explosion was also witnessed by other ships, and *Fusō* and *Mogami* promptly joined in the rescue efforts.

At the time of the explosion, *Mutsu* had a complement of about 1,500, but only 353 survived. Many of these survivors were petty officers and enlisted men who were engaged in deck operations, since there were few survivors among those who were inside the ship at the time of the explosion. The body of Captain Miyoshi Teruhiko was found in his cabin after a special diving operation.

Many of the survivors were on the deck at the time of the explosion and were able to jump into the sea immediately. However, a significant number of them sustained injuries to their legs due to the impact of the explosion, making it difficult for them to swim effectively. Additionally, there was a thick layer of heavy oil, reportedly up to 1 m thick in some places, spreading from *Mutsu*. Particularly for the injured, once they were engulfed by this layer, resurfacing was challenging. Despite managing to escape into the sea, many still perished.

Care for the injured was conducted with great caution. The occurrence of a large number of injuries at once would be evidence of a significant event. Therefore, after receiving initial treatment at the Kure Naval Hospital, they were sent to Mitsukojima for further treatment. Located in the most critical section within the naval base, communication with the outside world was strictly restricted, making it an ideal location for maintaining secrecy. Subsequently, the wounded were dispersed to various hospitals across the country, disguised as battlefield casualties, to maintain confidentiality.

The deceased were cremated on a small uninhabited island called Zokushima near Hashirajima, close to *Mutsu*. The task of cremation was carried out by the survivors of *Mutsu*. Perhaps the higher-ups judged that entrusting them with this task would prevent the leakage of information about the sinking, and they would handle the remains of their fallen comrades with particular care. The remains were not immediately handed over to the families but, instead, continued to receive payment for a while, as if the deceased were still alive. The notifications of death were sent to the families gradually and inconspicuously to avoid drawing attention.

Accidents involving ammunition explosions or main turret explosions on warships, while not common, are not particularly rare either. The IJN experienced several such incidents, and even after the sinking of *Mutsu*, a commission of inquiry led by Admiral Shiozawa Kōichi was established. This commission suspected deliberate human actions, such as arson, rather than spontaneous combustion.

However, the crew members of *Mutsu* along with *Nagato* were selected from individuals with good conduct records. While the possibility of sabotage by spies or rebels couldn't be completely ruled out, it was still considered unlikely. On the other hand, theft incidents had occurred on board *Mutsu* at the time, and the investigation into this matter was nearing its conclusion. It was speculated that this might be related to the explosion. However, the investigation did not provide conclusive evidence to confirm that the act was deliberate sabotage.

Furthermore, there were suspicions of spontaneous combustion accidents involving type 3 shells. If such a defect were inherent in these shells, it would necessitate alerting the entire navy. Therefore, thorough testing was conducted, but once again the results showed no evidence of any wrongdoing.

As a result, the cause of *Mutsu*'s sinking remains unknown to this day, even after parts of the ship were salvaged. Furthermore, Vice Admiral Shimizu Mitsumi, who was the commander of the 1st Fleet at the time, was relieved of his command and placed into reserve in February 1944, facing responsibility for the incident.

Mutsu's loss was to remain a secret, and survivors who narrowly escaped death were promptly sent to the southern regions, where communication with mainland Japan was difficult, without even being granted leave to visit their families. When they were initially sent away, the situation of the war was not yet dire, but many of them perished in their assigned posts later as the war situation deteriorated.

In the end, the sinking of the *Mutsu* was never publicly announced during the war, and the general public remained unaware of it until after the war. However, in reality, rumors about the incident had been circulating as "highly plausible rumors" since shortly after the accident. It is even said that in areas close to the scene, it had become somewhat of an open secret.

Furthermore, the navy had intentions to salvage and refurbish the *Mutsu* immediately after the sinking. However, due to the extensive damage, this plan was ultimately abandoned.

Human remains were salvaged after the war, and the Fukada Salvage Company acquired the salvage rights to the wreck in 1970. Large-scale salvage operations were then carried out for eight years, and part of *Mutsu*'s wreck and artifacts can be observed at the museum in Tōwa Chō.[1]

Nagato at the Battle for Leyte Gulf (*Shō Ichi Gō Sakusen*)

After participation in the Mariana Sea Battle, *Nagato* returned to Hashirajima anchorage on June 24, 1944, via Nakagusuku Bay (Okinawa) and proceeded to Kure on the twenty-seventh, where the navy yard, besides others, greatly strengthened the close-range antiaircraft (AA) defense weapons and fitted two surface and two air search radars.

The first mission after the departure on July 8 was to transport soldiers and material to Okinawa, followed by an almost uninterrupted training period at Lingga anchorage before the alert of Operation Victory One (*Shō Ichi Gō Sakusen*)[2] was issued on October 17 at 08:09 and was followed by the activation order on the eighteenth at 17:32.

Nagato was assigned to Battleship Division 1, which was part of the 1st Night Battle Force, composed of the 1st Squadron (battleships *Yamato*, *Musashi*, *Nagato*), 4th Squadron (heavy cruisers *Atago*, *Takao*, *Chōkai*, *Maya*), and 2nd Destroyer Squadron (light cruiser *Noshiro*, nine destroyers). This Night Battle Force was part of the First Diversion Attack Force (*Dai Ichi Yūgekitai*, 1YB), commanded by the commander in chief, Vice Admiral Kurita Takeo.[3] The commander of the 1st Squadron was Vice Admiral Ugaki Matome, former chief of staff of the Combined Fleet.

The 1YB departed Lingga anchorage on the eighteenth at 01:00 and entered Brunei Bay (west coast of Borneo) on the twentieth at 12:00. The ships replenished quickly, and the last operation conference with the commanding officers was held.

At that time, the annihilation of the invasion convoy and the landing forces was the primary operation goal of the 1YB, and a battle with surface forces was "accepted" only to the extent that it should enable the 1YB to penetrate the landing area. This situation was comparable to that of Vice Admiral Mikawa Gun'ichi, whose primary target was also the transports and landing forces, which he did not attack in favor of the screening forces (Battle of Savo Island in August 1942). Attack on cargo ships was much disliked and had caused considerable arguments between the 1YB and the Combined Fleet, culminating in this answer from Captain Kami Shigenori, staff of the Combined Fleet: "If the Philippines will be seized by the enemy, the shipping lane to the south will be completely cut off and Japan will die of thirst [that is, not obtaining its full supply]. Then the possession of the fleet is useless. The Philippines may not be lost. There will be no regret even if the Combined Fleet is also annihilated. . . . The war is in its last stage now." On the basis of the arguments of Rear Admiral Koyanagi Tomiji, chief of staff of 2nd Fleet, "The annihilation of the enemy main force should be the primary goal. If we have to assault the enemy harbor bay and to annihilate the transport ships, by all means we shall perform this duty. However, is the headquarters of the Combined Fleet prepared to accept that the surface force will be annihilated?"

Nagato at around 12:00 on October 21, 1944, at Brunei. This photo was taken by Lieutenant Shiraishi Tōbei from the destroyer *Isokaze* while she was moving within the anchorage to refuel.

Nagato preparing for battle at around 12:00 on October 21, 1944, at Brunei (Borneo), in a photo taken by Lieutenant Shiraishi Tōbei, torpedo officer aboard the destroyer *Isokaze*. With the order for Operation *Shō 1*, preparations for the decisive battle for the survival of the empire was complete. Refueling is also complete, and the ships in the distance are, from the left, the battleships *Yamato* and *Musashi* and the heavy cruiser *Mogami*.

OPERATIONAL HISTORIES

Advance

In response to the Combined Fleet DesOpOrd[4] #363 (SMS 200813), the 1YB main force departed Brunei on the twenty-second at 08:05 to the almost-1,200-mile-distant landing point. The route was along the Palawan Channel and Mindoro Strait, most dangerous from the viewpoint of submarine attacks, then Tablas Strait and passing through Sibuyan Sea, where concentrated air attacks against the advancing ships had to be expected. After that, the 1YB had to pass through the San Bernardino Strait (the strongest current was 8 mph), then along the east coast of Samar Island and into the Leyte Gulf. This route was considered advantageous because it was outside the reconnaissance area of the US planes stationed at Morotai. Therefore, the detection by carrier-based planes might be delayed until the last phase of the approach.

That the "Dangerous Ground" correctly bore this name became evident on the twenty-third, when the US submarines *Darter* and *Dace* attacked the main force heading northeast along the west coast of Palawan Island. The heavy cruisers *Atago* (Kurita's flagship) and *Maya* each received four torpedo hits and sank quickly. The heavy cruiser *Takao* was hit by two torpedoes and was so heavily damaged that it had to return to Brunei, escorted by two destroyers.

The main force, now reduced to twenty-seven ships, advanced through the Mindoro Strait, headed south of Mindoro Island, and entered the Tablas Strait, continually reacting to "phantom submarine" alarms.

Alerted by the report of the two US submarines about the detection of the Japanese force (1YB main force), TF 38, then in the area off Luzon Island, was ordered to reconnoiter a vast sea area early in the morning of the twenty-fourth. Using a total of 107 planes, the Japanese warships, advancing in two ring formations (defense formation Y 25 against air attacks taken at 07:47), were detected when rounding the southern part of Mindoro Island and advancing into the Sibuyan Sea.

Nagato, part of the first ring formation and positioned at the left flank and aft of the battleship *Yamato*,[5] was identified and reported as a heavy cruiser by the US observers, which was a considerable misidentification.

The main force of the 1YB was shadowed until 09:10, which was one hour after the lookouts on *Yamato* had detected the "Charley" in bearing 10 degrees, range 50 km. The main force was between Mindoro Island and Tablas Island and made headway with a speed of 18 knots and zigzagging.

The main force of Vice Admiral Kurita Takeo's fleet departing Brunei in line-ahead (*tanjūjin*) formation on October 22, 1944. *From the right*, the ships are *Nagato, Musashi, Yamato* (all from the 1st Squadron), and in front of them are the heavy cruiser groups from the 4th Squadron (*Atago, Takao, Chōkai, Maya*) and the 5th Squadron (*Myōkō, Haguro*).

Consecutive Air Battles

The 1YB planned to advance under the protection of the land-based air force but was forced to head for the landing point without an air umbrella and became the target of consecutive air attacks, which brought it into an emergency situation. Air support was requested repeatedly but was not received, because the land-based air force had been almost annihilated.

First Attack

At 10:15, the lookouts on *Nagato* reported a lonely B-24 130 degrees at port. Rear Admiral Kōbe Yūji,[6] who had taken over command from Rear Admiral Hayakawa Mikio on December 15, 1943, ordered, "Clear for action!"

The main force increased their speed to fourth battle speed (22 knots). However, the Liberator bomber did not attack but opened range bearing 110 degrees to port of *Nagato* and disappeared in the clouds. With no immediate danger in sight, the commanding officer issued, "Rest at battle stations!" Enemy air attacks were certain because the main force had been detected twice

One minute later, the lookouts on *Nagato* reported a large group of planes bearing 85 degrees to port, and Kōbe ordered, "Air battle!"[7] *Nagato* observed forty-one enemy planes to starboard 100 degrees, distance approximately 20,000 m, and noticed that they began to divide into three groups.

One minute later, one group of about twelve planes was seen to starboard 84 degrees and range about 15,000 m, flying to port direction. The chief gunnery officer, Inoue Takeo, who was in the air command station, ordered, "Main and secondary guns commence fire on the enemy planes to starboard!" and "Independent firing!" The buzzer for air defense rang. At 10:27, *Nagato* commenced fire. Her main guns also fired type 3 incendiary projectiles like *Yamato*, which had commenced fire one minute earlier. The Japanese ships lacked radar-directed fire control and had to rely upon optical gear.

Taking *Nagato* as their target, four SB2Cs each released one 454 kg AP and SAP and two common bombs. They reported two hits and one probable hit, but actually no direct hits were obtained. At 10:29, two bombs detonated close to the starboard bow. The enemy planes opened range to port at 10:32. But one minute later, *Nagato*'s lookouts reported eight TBMs to port 10 degrees, and her commanding officer outmaneuvered this attack by turning to port. However, the TBMs attacked other ships, prominent of which were *Yamato* and *Musashi*.

The first air attack ended at 10:47, when the last planes disappeared on the horizon, but no attack was recorded after 10:40, and the end of the air alert was issued.

Second Attack

At 11:54 the battleship *Musashi* detected an unknown group of aircraft bearing 200 degrees, range 10,000 m. Ten minutes later, at 12:04, the lookouts on *Nagato* reported a group of about twenty-eight dive-bombers to starboard bearing 88 degrees, range 10,000 m. This was the second air attack group from the carrier *Intrepid*, consisting of thirty-one planes. The chief gunnery officer gave the main guns permission to fire, and *Nagato*'s 40 cm guns fired a few type 0 common projectiles (*Rei Shiki tsūjōdan*), which were almost useless against planes, before again changing to type 3 incendiary projectiles.

At 12:08, a SB2C released a 454 kg AP bomb on *Nagato* that evaded a hit by turning full to port. The enemy plane passed her flying obliquely to port in the direction of the stern.

At 12:18, *Nagato*'s chief gunnery officers ordered, "Cease fire!," and this was followed by "Rest at the battle stations!" The second air attack was over, and the air alert was canceled. The main body of the 1YB took course 90 degrees and reduced speed to first battle speed (16 knots).

Third Attack

At 13:21, *Nagato* discovered enemy planes bearing 255 degrees and ranges from 25,500 to 35,500 m. Three minutes later the main body turned to starboard because the enemy plane formations approached. After that, the planes disappeared from *Nagato*'s radar display.

This time, the majority of the attackers was ordered to attack the thirteen ships of the ring formation, in which two battleships of the Kongō class were prominent, while eight F6Fs and ten SB2Cs of the USS *Essex* group were ordered to attack the thirteen ships, among them two battleships of the Yamato class and *Nagato*.

At 13:31, *Nagato* focused attention upon a formation of about forty dive-bombers flying to starboard at about 10,000 m distance. Because *Yamato* opened fire upon these planes, *Nagato*'s chief gunnery officer issued the order "Begin individual firing!," and some of the guns commenced firing.

At 13:45, *Nagato* spotted twenty torpedo bombers at a range of about 15,000 m and commenced fire against eight torpedo bombers approaching at bearing 20 degrees and closing range quickly. She was attacked by four TBMs but could evade the torpedoes by maneuvering and AA fire. When the torpedo bombers opened range with bearing 10 degrees, firing was ceased.

At 13:53, *Nagato* discovered a group of about twenty planes bearing 103 degrees to port, range approximately 30,000 m, and the order "Alert for air battle!" was given. Three planes approached from bearing 125 degrees, and when the range was reduced to 28,000 m, the aft main gun group received the firing order.[8]

At the same time, four SB2Cs (another source states four TBM-1Cs equipped with bombs instead of torpedoes) each released two 454 kg AP and SAP bombs on *Nagato*, and the pilots reported three hits. However, no bomb hit, and *Nagato* remained undamaged.

Fourth Attack
Nagato reduced speed to 16 knots (first battle speed) at 14:11. Five minutes later, a large group of aircraft were seen to starboard 30 degrees, range approximately 25,000 m, and "Air battle!" was ordered. Thirteen planes were detected approaching from starboard 2 degrees, and the speed was increased to third battle speed (20 knots).

At 14:22 the main guns of *Nagato* commenced firing upon the planes approaching from starboard. The group separated into two formations when the range was reduced to about 20,000 m, and approached from different bearings (2 and 31 degrees). At 14:25 the chief gunnery officer ordered, "Individual gunfight!" against the group coming from starboard 30 degrees.

When the range was closed to the effective firing range of the 25 mm machine guns, they opened fire. However, most of these close-range AA weapons were triple and single mounts with gun side aim and no fire director. Therefore, only a few bullets hit the well-protected targets, which were rarely brought down by a few hits. The lack of fire directors was the principal reason why so few enemy planes were shot down.

At 14:26, *Nagato* became the target of four bomb-armed F6Fs. Four 227 kg common bombs detonated close to starboard near the bow. Between frames 24 and 25, about seven hundred holes, small and large, appeared in the outer plating. They were closed with wooden plugs, but it took forty-eight hours before all holes were closed and made tight.[9] The enemy planes retired at 14:48, 70 degrees to port, and disappeared in the clouds after two minutes.

At 14:56, *Nagato*'s chief gunnery officer ordered, "Cease fire!," followed by the order "Stand by at the station!" The fourth attack ended.

Fifth Attack
Five minutes later, the battleship *Kongō*, part of the second ring formation, opened fire upon enemy planes.

At 15:03, *Nagato*'s commanding officer ordered fifth battle speed (24 knots), when reports about the sighting of more enemy planes at a range of 27,000 m arrived. One group, identified as "nine dive-bombers, seven torpedo bombers, and five fighters are flying to right," another "large group of planes to starboard 130 degrees moves to right," and "from port, 72 degrees planes are approaching." *Nagato*'s main guns opened fire, directed upon the latter group.

At 15:14, enemy dive-bombers approached *Nagato* from port 10 degrees, range 15,000 m, whereupon the chief gunnery officer ordered, "Begin individual firing!" Two minutes later, twenty-five planes approached from starboard and began their 50-degree dive. Kōbe ordered a hard turn to port to outmaneuver them.

Seven SB2Cs of the carrier *Franklin* and eight F6Fs attacked *Nagato*. The dive-bombers released twelve 227 kg AP bombs from a height of 600 m and claimed four hits and two near misses. The bomb-armed fighters released seven 456 kg SAP bombs from approximately 900 m and reported two near misses. Two of the nineteen bombs were hits. One bomb hit the ship's boat deck about amidships. The detonation damaged the ventilation system for the no. 1 boiler room slightly and destroyed the access ways to the no. 2 and no. 4 secondary guns. Three secondary guns were put out of action. The support of the no. 2 12.7 cm high-angle gun was slightly lifted by the detonation gases, so that the gun could no longer be trained. However, the latter damage was repaired after one hour by cutting deck plates of the emplacement, because the operation of the gun was urgently necessary.[10]

The second bomb penetrated the skylight of the galley for enlisted men,[11] detonated in the aft part of the communication room, and destroyed radio, telephone, and code equipment. Due to the destruction of the communication equipment, the communication within the ship and to other ships broke down. Several men of the damage control parties dispatched to this room received electric shocks by the cutting of electric cables, which had become wet by the foregoing firefighting.

These two bombs caused the biggest damage *Nagato* received on October 24. The personnel losses were considerably high: in total, 158 men were killed or wounded—52 killed in action, 20 severely wounded, and 86 slightly wounded.

Among the other bombs, three were near misses, and their splinters increased the number of holes in the hull plating and elsewhere. The effect of hammocks and rope mantlets as protection against detonation gases and splinters was estimated to be of great value in case of these bomb hits.

Due to the damage of the ventilation system of the no. 1 boiler room, the boiler could no longer be operated, and Kōbe decided for three-shaft propulsion by accepting the proposal of the chief engineer. As a consequence, *Nagato*'s maximum speed temporarily dropped to 22 knots. However, after repair the boiler went into operation again. With four-shaft propulsion and all boilers making steam, her speed was no longer impaired.

At 15:34 the chief gunnery officer of *Nagato* ordered, "Cease fire!" The fifth and last air attack of this day ended.

Nagato during antiaircraft combat in the Battle of Leyte Gulf on October 24, 1944. It appears to be an image taken right after the forward main gun turrets fired type 3 shells. After returning to Yokosuka after the Battle of Leyte Gulf, *Nagato* remained in port, reportedly due to fuel shortages. *US Navy*

Operations on October 25

On October 25 at 00:35, the 1YB, now reduced from thirty-one to twenty-three ships but still showing an impressive firepower with four battleships, six heavy cruisers, two light cruisers, and eleven destroyers, passed through San Bernardino Strait[12] and took course to the rendezvous point with the third TG (the Nishimura force, which was totally annihilated in the Surigao Strait before dawn on the twenty-fifth) in the sea area east of Suluan Island lighthouse and proceeded south along the east coast of Samar Island.

At 06:17, ten minutes before sunrise, the order "Prepare for air attack!" was issued, and the ships were about to change from the night formation to the ring formation when, at 06:23, the radar of *Yamato* indicated enemy planes off the bow, range 50,000 m, and at 06:40 the heavy cruiser *Kumano* (7th Squadron) opened fire upon two planes.

At 06:41, lookouts on *Nagato* reported the sighting of masts on the horizon (escort carriers of "Taffy 3"), and all men took to the battle stations. Seven minutes later the order for AA fighting was given, and the guns opened fire against four planes approaching from port 59 degrees, range 18,000 m. But the AA fire was stopped after three minutes, and at 06:51 the main gun battle was ordered by "Gun battle to port!" and "Maximum speed!"

After *Yamato* had fired a salvo from both forward main gun turrets, *Nagato* also fired salvos from the two forward turrets against three enemy carriers visible 63 degrees to port at the end of the squall, taking the water columns of *Yamato*'s 46 cm projectiles as auxiliary aiming points. The range to the targets was 32,800 m. Because both ships had prepared for air attack, the first and second salvos were type 3 incendiary shells, but from the third salvo, AP projectiles were fired.

Four water columns emerged a little forward of the bow of USS St. Lo. The distance to the ship was about 180 m. These projectiles were probably fired from Nagato, accompanying the flagship.[13] The projectiles of the second salvo hit at about the same distance. Like their seven escorts, the six escort carriers laid frequent smoke screens and retired into the squall to prevent the Japanese from sighting them. It was an effective method in case of using optical fire control, and since accuracy and reliability of the modified type 22 radar of the Japanese vessels used for radar-controlled firing left much to be desired, the goal was attained.

Kurita judged the escort carriers to be large carriers of a "fast TF."[14] He wanted to annihilate them as quickly as possible and ordered an assault attack of the battleships. Yamato and Nagato operated as one unit, and the latter also accompanied the former at the much-criticized escape movement to the north for about 10 miles to avoid torpedoes launched by the destroyer Heermann.

The chasing battle of the surface force lasted for about two a half hours, and before Kurita made his most controversial decision and ordered his ships to successively join the flagship.[15] This order meant the stop of the chasing battle at the moment the destruction of the escort carriers was almost certain, because the condition of the US Taffies had become hopeless. The surprise of the American commanders may be expressed as "Unbelievable!"

Because Nagato accompanied Yamato, the number of projectiles fired by the main and secondary guns was smaller than in the other capital ships, as is shown in the next table.

The following table shows Nagato's ammunition expenditure from October 23 to 25, broken down according to the types of projectiles and for all guns.

Table 20: Ammunition Expenditure, October 23–25, 1944		
Ship	Main guns	Secondary guns
BB Nagato	41 cm – 45	14 cm – 92
BB Yamato	46 cm – 104	15.5 cm – 127
BB Kongō	36 cm – 211	15 cm – 177
BB Haruna	36 cm – 95	15 cm – 255
CA Haguro	20 cm – 581	-----
CA Tone	20 cm – 420	-----
CL Yahagi	15 cm – 334	-----
DD Urakaze	12.7 cm – 347	-----

Note:
BB = Battleship; CA = Heavy cruiser; CL = Light cruiser; DD = Destroyer.

Table 21: Ammunition Expenditure of Nagato, October 23–25, 1944			
41 cm	14 cm	12.7 cm	25 mm
Type 1 AP Model 4 – 45	-----	----	----
Type 0 Common – 52	Capped Common Mod. 2 – 92	Common – 1,502	Common – 35,209
Type 3 Incendiary – 84	No. 2 Common (red) – 41	Incendiary – 38	Tracer – 12,327
	Type 0 Common – 520		
Total: 181	668	1,540	47,536

As a result, the sinking of four aircraft carriers, three heavy cruisers, and three destroyers, plus damage of two aircraft carriers and two to three heavy cruisers or destroyers, was claimed. The actual losses on the American side were one escort carrier and four destroyers sunk. Fifteen 20.3 cm projectiles hit the escort carrier *Kalinin Bay*. Because type 91 AP projectiles, designed to penetrate heavy armor, were fired, the projectiles penetrated the hull without detonation and only punctured it. Tankers and other types of merchant ships were converted to escort carriers, and these ships had no protection.

Retreat

The assembly of the ships took about one and a half hours. Then, the force headed for the entrance to Leyte Gulf. Kurita knew from the report received on the twenty-fourth at 02:00 that eighty transport ships were inside Leyte Gulf. However, this was one and a half days earlier, and he did not know whether these ships were still in the bay. So, he thought that the decisive battle with the US TF to the north would be more effective than to penetrate Leyte Gulf.

At 12:30 he reported to the commander in chief of the Combined Fleet, Admiral Toyota Soemu, his decision to give up the assault operation of the Leyte anchorage and proceed north instead along the east coast of Samar Island to pass San Bernardino Strait after the decisive battle with the enemy TF.

At the time of the report, thirty-five Avengers and thirty-five Wildcat fighters had sighted the 1YB and attacked about fifteen minutes later. While Morison[16] states one bomb, Ugaki Matome[17] states two bomb hits, of which one pierced the anchor deck while the other hit a roller and detonated outboard, leaving holes in the bows. According to Ugaki, there were still numerous holes by splinters and aft.

Prior to this, the type 0 reconnaissance plane of *Nagato* (transhipped from *Yamato*) reported the presence of forty transport ships in the Leyte Gulf at 12:30. Kurita received this information aboard his flagship at 13:20, when the remnants of the main force turned to the north. However, irrespective of the presence of a sufficient number of vulnerable ships in Leyte Gulf, he did not change his opinion and gave up the Leyte Gulf assault operation, the central operation within Operation Victory One. It is very hard to understand Kurita's decisions at this "decisive operation."

Colonel Hattori Takushirō, of Imperial General Headquarters, Army Section, Operation Division, in his four-volume *The Complete History of the Greater East Asia War* (*Daitōa Sensō Zenshi*), criticized that Vice Admiral Kurita gave up the essential operation (annihilation of the transport ships in Leyte Gulf) after carrying out the "suppression operation" against the enemy TF and high-handedly took course to the north, while Vice Admiral Ozawa Jisaburō sacrificed his own force to lure the enemy north and offered Kurita the chance to fulfill the primary goal of the operation.

During the retreat, the 1YB was also attacked on October 26 by carrier-based torpedo bombers and US Army B-24s. *Nagato* responded with her main and secondary guns, using mainly type 3 incendiary projectiles, and claimed several planes shot down. She suffered no damage by these attacks.

There were no more attacks on the twenty-seventh, and the remnants arrived at Brunei on the twenty-eighth and refueled.

Use as a Stationary Antiaircraft Defense Ship

After an attack by US Army B-24s on November 16, the battleship group (*Yamato*, *Nagato*, *Kongō*) escorted by destroyers and the light cruiser *Noshiro* departed Brunei Bay for the homeland on the next day. En route, *Kongō* became the victim of torpedoes launched by USS *Sealion II* (SS-215) on the twenty-first, but *Nagato* entered Yokosuka naval port on the twenty-fifth. She was drydocked for the repair of the battle damages and for preparations to serve as a stationary floating antiaircraft battery, despite the fact that due to the lack of sufficient power (i.e., lack of fuel prevented the operation of boilers and generators), her AA guns were not fully operable. Besides adding 25 mm machine guns, the removal of the funnel and the upper part of the mainmast to expand firing-arc protection by camouflage and torpedo nets was part of the preparations.

Half a year passed with *Nagato* stationed inactive and immobilized in port due to lack of fuel[18] before IJN's operable battleships (*Nagato*, *Ise*, *Hyūga*, *Haruna*) were assigned to the Special Guard Fleet on June 1, 1945. In company with it, *Nagato* was stripped of her secondary guns and also half of her 12.7 cm twin high-angle guns, which were installed on land in expectation of future landings and air attacks. The crew was reduced and the camouflage was greatly reinforced.

However, camouflage did not prevent her from being attacked when TF 58 launched massive air attacks on Yokosuka naval base on July 18, with *Nagato*, the biggest ship in Tokyo Bay, as primary target. An almost helpless target against the mass of carrier-based aircraft, she was hit by only two 224 kg GP bombs (with instantaneous fuses) and one rocket, the latter a dud. The investigation by the US Naval Technical Mission to Japan (*S-06-1*, pp. 8–13 and plate 1) noted no internal damage or flooding and assumed that her underwater hull had not been ruptured by near misses.[19]

The first bomb hit the bridge structure below the navigation bridge and above the roof of the conning tower. While fragments only scarred the latter, the navigation bridge was greatly destroyed, and thirteen officers (among them her commanding and executive officers) were killed. With the main portion of the blast and fragmentation directed upward, the irregular hole in the deck of the navigation bridge had a diameter of about 4 m. Fire did not break out.

The second bomb pierced the shelter deck aft of the mainmast to port and detonated near the barbette of the third main gun turret and the upper deck. There was no fire, and the effect upon fighting efficiency was almost negligible, even though "four light 25-mounts on the upper deck were rendered inoperable." However, again there were personnel losses.

The (supposedly) 12.7 cm rocket hit the fantail to port, passed the admiral's cabin (the investigator discovered a scratch about 5 cm deep and 24 cm long at the port edge of the table), and exited the hull to starboard.

Generally speaking, the damage inflicted on *Nagato* was slight in view of her condition and must have been a grave disappointment for the attackers, should they have known it. However, as predicted by Captain Kami the previous year, the war was in its last stage, and *Nagato* was handed over to the Allied forces on August 30, 1945, and removed from the list on September 15. It was roughly twenty-five years after her commissioning as the most powerful battleship of the IJN.

Nagato in Tokyo Bay in September–December 1945. To the right is the high-speed transport USS *Horace A. Bass* (APD-124). On March 30, 1945, four 14 cm guns were removed, and the remaining secondary guns had been removed by April 23. Two twin 12.7 cm high-angle gun mounts were added in January 1945, but all 12.7 cm guns and fire control systems were landed in July. When *Nagato* was surrendered, her antiaircraft outfit consisted of only forty-five 25 mm machine guns (9 × 3 + 3 × 2 + 12 × 1) with associated fire control systems. The type 21 radar was removed on February 4, as was part of the type 13 radar. The type 22 radar remained until the end, and the remainder of the type 13 was probably removed when the aft superstructure was cut down. It is uncertain when the catapult was removed, but most likely on June 1, when the funnel and aft superstructure were cut down for camouflage purposes.

On July 25, 1946, at Bikini Atoll, a historic photograph captures the moment of an underwater nuclear explosion. From the size of *Nagato* in the foreground, one can imagine the enormity of the water column. During this experiment, *Nagato* was positioned 1,000 m from the epicenter of the explosion, resulting in a small hole in the bottom of the hull toward starboard aft. A few hours later, the ship developed an approximate 5-degree list, but the increase was very gradual, and the ship remained afloat. However, on the early morning of the fifth day of the experiment, July 30, *Nagato* was no longer visible on the water's surface. *The Maru Special*

CHAPTER 14
Who Designed the Nagato Class?

Lieutenant (shipbuilding) Hiraga Yuzuru became a member of the Navy Technical Department on February 3, 1909, and from the next day worked in the 3rd Division (Shipbuilding), the chief of which was Fukuda Umanosuke, the father of Fukuda Keiji, who is famous as the chief designer of the Yamato class. Hiraga was involved in the basic design of the Fusō class.

On August 5, 1912, he became a member of the Shipbuilding Department of Yokosuka Navy Yard and was dismissed from the lectures in the technical course of Tokyo Imperial University, which he had begun on September 25, 1909.

On August 26, 1912, he was made the chief of the drawing factory and was in charge of the newly built battleship *Yamashiro*, the battle cruiser *Hiei*, and the destroyer *Kaba*.

On June 10, 1913, he also became chief of the Shipbuilding Factory of Yokosuka Navy Yard and had to execute both functions.

On November 14, 1913, he delivered a lecture to the Shipbuilding Association about the use of special steel in recent warships and received a prize for it on October 23, 1915.

In the meantime, he acted as a member of the trial committees of the previously mentioned ships *Hiei* in February 1914 and *Kaba* in February 1915, and he also became a member of the committee of the fiftieth anniversary of the founding of the Yokosuka Navy Yard on September 22, 1915.

On November 3, 1915, *Yamashiro* was launched, and on January 26, 1916, the opening ceremony of the great dock of Yokosuka Navy Yard was another highlight.

On April 7, 1916, Hiraga was dismissed from the dual duty as chief of the Shipbuilding Factory and was moved to the Navy Technical Department (then *Kaigun Gijutsu Honbu*) as superintendent of shipbuilding on May 15, 1916. He was ordered to work in the 4th Division (Shipbuilding), with Fukuda Umanosuke as chief and Asaoka Mitsutoshi as chief of the Basic Design Section. From that time, he was in charge of the basic design of the capital ships of the Eight-Eight Fleet.

Prior to this, the building of *Nagato* had been ordered from Kure Navy Yard on May 12, 1916, three days before Hiraga was moved to the Navy Technical Department from Yokosuka Navy Yard. Therefore, it is certain that Hiraga was not the designer of the Nagato class, as is often stated.

On May 31–June 1, 1916, the Jutland sea battle was fought, and on August 11,[1] Hiraga submitted the modified design of the *Nagato* (A 114), based on the war lessons of Jutland, as a member of the Temporary Investigation Committee. The navy minister ordered its execution on October 28, 1916. Consequently, it is certain that he made small modifications regarding protection and speed.

After that, a large number of designs of high-speed battleships and battle cruisers were worked out, all adopting inclined hull side armor and mounting 16" guns, with the number increased to ten from the original eight from basic design A 119 onward.

In January 1917, he became a member of the investigation committee of the battle cruiser *Tsukuba*'s explosion (chairman, Rear Admiral Katō Hiroharu, also known as Katō Kanji; report submitted on July 23), was promoted to captain on April 1, 1917, and proposed the so-called "Modified *Mutsu* design" on June 12, 1917.

On July 14, 1917, the budget of the Eight-Four Fleet passed the Diet. On July 26, the former chief of the Basic Design Section, Asaoka Mitsutoshi,[2] became the chief of the 4th Division, and Yamamoto Kaizō took over his former post and function.

On December 1, 1920, Yamamoto was promoted to chief of the 4th Division, and Captain Hiraga was ordered to be the chief of the Basic Design Section. He was promoted to rear admiral on June 1, 1922, and was dismissed from his post on October 1, 1923, with the order to visit Europe and the United States to investigate the shipbuilding situation after the conclusion of the Washington Treaty. His dismissal was triggered by controversies with the naval general staff about the fitting of torpedo tubes in the Myōkō class, but it was only one example of his resistance to requirements if he deemed them not proper to a design.

Before that, on August 13, 1923, Vice Admiral Yamamoto had been replaced by Suzuki Keiji as chief of the 4th Division of the Navy Technical Department. Therefore, Hiraga was the only chief of the Basic Design Section who was not promoted to the chief of the 3rd/4th Division, and it is said he regretted it all his life.

From the foregoing summary, the following conclusions may be drawn:

- Hiraga was not the designer of the Nagato class (he worked in Yokosuka Navy Yard from August 5, 1912, to May 14, 1916), but he made modifications based on the lessons drawn from the Jutland sea battle (July–August 1916).
- The initial design of the *Nagato* was almost certainly made by Yamamoto Kaizō under the direction of Asaoka Mitsutoshi, and it was completed in 1915, the year prior to the construction order.
- Hiraga's completely revised design for *Nagato*'s sister, *Mutsu*, was rejected.
- Hiraga was never chief of the 4th Division of the Navy Technical Department.

Endnotes

Chapter 2
1. For a more thorough discussion about the origins of the Eight-Eight Fleet, see Hans Lengerer's *Outline History of the Imperial Japanese Navy, 1868–1945* (Zagreb, Croatia: Despot Infinitus, 2021).

Chapter 3
1. Navy Minister Yashiro Rokurō resigned in August 1915 for assuming responsibility for the bribery scandal with Interior Minister Ōura Kanetake at the center, and Vice Admiral Katō, known as an advocate of the "big ships, big guns" principle, took over. Immediately afterward, the realization of the Eight-Eight Fleet began with the proposal to carry out the first stage.
2. The correct rank of Yamamoto was *zōsen daikan*, but in September 1919 this was changed to *zōsen daisa* (shipbuilding captain). At that time, Yamamoto had been promoted to rear admiral, and he retired from the navy with the rank of vice admiral.

Chapter 4
1. With the limitation of the vertical and horizontal armor to the vital part, the so-called concentrated protection was adopted. This system was perfected in the Kaga class by the adoption of the inclined belt armor and was a feature of Hiraga's capital ship designs, set forth in his *Kongō* replacement design, which created a sensation due to Hiraga's unprecedented behavior, and was also realized in the design of the Yamato class, when acting as an adviser to Fukuda Keiji.
2. This could not be permitted, since it would have retarded the construction schedule for about one year and had made useless most of the preparatory work.

Chapter 6
1. She was the second capital ship after the battleship *Fusō* built in that dock and was followed by the battle cruiser (later aircraft carrier) *Akagi* after the extension of the dock and the fortification of the cranes. In November 1937, the battleship *Yamato* was laid down here.

Chapter 7
1. Kaneda (1872–1925) is referred to as a weapon production officer (*zōhei shōkō*) in several postwar Japanese books, but on the basis of documents left by Vice Admiral Hiraga in the Tokyo University and describing the inventor and date of adoption, this is wrong. According to Fukui Shizuo, Kaneda was an "authority of gunnery techniques," and when he died in June 1925, he was a member of the 1st Division of the Navy Technical Department as well as a teacher at the Naval Academy. In addition, it is also said that the multipost mast was adopted before the start of the construction of *Nagato*, but this is also wrong on the basis of Hiraga's estate documents. Before the Pacific War, this fact was already published in the magazine *Senpaku*, but after the war it must have fallen into oblivion.

Chapter 8
1. *Kaigun Kikan-shi* (*History of Marine Engineering*), vol. 2, pp. 520–28; *Shōwa Zōsen-shi*, pp. 664–72; *Kaigun Zōsen Gijutsu Gaiyō*, vol. 7, pp. 1671–72, 1758.
2. The Navy Technical Department (NTD, *Kaigun Kansei Honbu*) was separated into a technical (*Kaigun Gijutsu Honbu* = Gihon) and administrative Warship Equipment Division (*Kaigun Kanseibu*) from October 1, 1915, until September 30, 1920, due

to the so-called Siemens affair (*shimensu jiken*, a bribery case). The two branches were subsequently again combined.

3. Each of the oil-fired boilers generated sufficient steam for 4,450 shp, making a total of 66,750 shp. The mixed-firing boilers generated steam for 2,200 shp, making a total of 13,250 shp.

4. Gear cutting was a problem in the IJN for a considerable time. Teeth-cutting machines were imported from England (David Brown & Sons) and then Germany (e.g., Reinecker), but it took until the end of the 1930s before the quality was satisfactory.

5. According to *Kaigun Kikan-shi*, p. 526, *Nagato*'s LPTs were not at first equipped with this free gear type, while *Mutsu*'s LPTs had it. However, comparative experiments proved the saving of 10 percent fuel in case of *Mutsu*. On the basis of this result, the gears for *Nagato*'s LPTs were fitted later.

Chapter 9

1. At that time, four ships of the Fusō class were to be built.

2. Two longitudinal flash-tight bulkheads were fitted between the guns with about a 0.5 m distance between them, providing passage from one side of the gunhouse to the other only by means of flash-tight doors through these bulkheads. The working chamber was also divided longitudinally in a similar manner. It deserves particular attention that the post for the turret trainer in the working chamber was totally enclosed and comparatively soundproof (very important in view of order transmitting).

3. Report O-47(N)-1 states that both guns and turrets were produced in Kure and Muroran, but the latter could not be confirmed by the Japanese sources used by the authors.

4. Tokyo: Hara Shobō, 1977.

5. Readers interested in this topic should make reference the authors' *Battleship Tosa Demolition Tests to the Modified Yamato Class* (Zagreb, Croatia: Despot Infinitus, 2019), vol. 3 of *Capital Ships of the Imperial Japanese Navy, 1868–1945*, in which the fire control system is described in more detail on pp. 180–203. A history of earlier fire control systems in the IJN has been published in vol. 1, *Armourclad Fusō to Kongō Class Battle Cruisers*, pp. 556–78, in the same series.

Chapter 11

1. According to the *Guide Book of Nagato* (1929–30 edition), "The cooling wind in summertime and the warm air in winter season are supplied to every corner of the ship," but this should be considered from the time of the design, the living standard of the population, and the then-current value of habitability.

Chapter 13

1. For more about the loss of *Mutsu*, see Michael Williams, "Battleship *Mutsu*: An Investigation into Her Loss," in the authors' *Contributions to the History of Imperial Japanese Warships*, papers XVII–XX.

2. The IJN's "decisive battle plan" in case of an attack on the Philippines by US forces. Fundamentally, (1) attack the enemy task forces and transport vessels by the entire land-based air forces as soon as they approach, (2) lure the enemy main forces north by the Japanese carriers approaching from that direction, and (3) advance of the 1YB (1st Division Attack Force, *Dai 1 Yūgekitai*) to the enemy's landing point, to annihilate the landing force two days after the beginning of the enemy's landing operation.

3. 1YB was formed by a total of three night battle forces composed of seven battleships, eleven heavy cruisers, two light cruisers, and nineteen destroyers—a total of thirty-nine ships. These night battle forces resembled the USN task groups (TGs), of which the main force was composed of the First and Second TGs (the Kurita Force was composed of five battleships, ten heavy cruisers, two light cruisers, and fifteen destroyers), and the support force (Vice Admiral Nishimura Shōji) as the third TG.

4. Dispatch operational order.

5. The authors' *Battleship Tosa Demolition Tests to the Modified Yamato Class* contains maps of this and other formations and track charts based on the battle diaries and *Senshi Sōsho*, vol. 56.

6. Promoted to rear admiral on October 15, 1944.

7. The weather conditions were as follows: air pressure 758.68 mm Hg, temperature 32°C, wind direction 320 degrees, wind speed 8.0 m/second, clear, amount of clouds 4, wave height 1 m, sight 30 km.

8. The sighting of twenty planes at both 13:45 and 13:53 is somewhat suspect and may be an error. Should the planes releasing the bombs at 13:53 have been TBM-1Cs instead of SB2C-3s, the second sighting might be an error.

9. The DAR (detailed action record) enumerates the holes in the hull sides and important positions to about nine hundred (including splinters received by three near misses received later) and refers to the seriousness of damages, which could be caused by near misses.

10. In the DAR of *Nagato*, the doubling of the high-angle guns by mounting four twins at one hull side and also the fire control system is required. In addition, the too-slow training of the high-angle guns was particularly pointed out in case planes attacked from the bow or stern direction, when the arc of fire also became a problem.

11. The destruction of the galley for ratings caused a problem. The crew was hungry because the subsequent air attacks had not permitted them to leave the stations and take a meal, and in the DAR an increase of the number of galleys for ratings is recommended.

12. The much-criticized orders of Kurita to reverse course and other tasks are not taken up here.

13. *Nagato*'s DAR records a hit on an escort carrier, causing the ship to smoke heavily and other visual effects, but this must have been confused with a smoke screen, since no hit is recorded on the American side.

14. This estimation is quite incomprehensible and is supposed to have been stated as one of the many attempts to cover up the true reasons of Kurita's decisions on that day.

15. The reasons given in the DAR and elsewhere—namely, fuel condition, assault of Leyte Gulf, etc.—seem to be more or less an excuse.

16. Samuel E. Morison, *History of United States Naval Operations in World War II*, vol. 12, *Leyte, June 1944–January 1945*, p. 308.

17. *Fading Victory: The Diary of Admiral Matome Ugaki, 1941–1945*, p. 500.

18. According to the US Naval Technical Mission to Japan, *S-06-1* (report), p. 8, a coal-burning donkey boiler was installed for furnishing steam to the galley, heating, etc.

19. This appears doubtful, because some compartments were flooded on the way to Eniwetok in 1946. Earlier, upon the inspection in September–October 1945 by the "new owners," holes in the double-bottom fuel tanks and the flooding by 2,000 tons of seawater were reported as a result of sixty near misses!

Chapter 14

1. In Naitō Hatsuho's *Hiraga Yuzuru ikōshū* ("Collection of posthumous manuscripts of Hiraga Yuzuru") (Tokyo: Shuppan Kyōdō-sha, 1985), p. 581, this date is given, but Hiraga in his "On the after-war development of the ships of the Imperial Navy" states, "About that time, the report of the Jutland engagement (July 1916) was received, and the result of a careful study of the lessons obtained in that great sea battle was to later influence the design by increasing the displacement, speed, and defensive power, and this new design was completed in September of the same year." In a lecture to the crown prince on December 18, 1924, Hiraga explained that the improved "design was adopted in September." Because no modification can be called "completed" before being adopted, it may be supposed that Hiraga had completed the changes in August, the Higher Technical Conference adopted it in September, and the navy minister ordered its execution in October.

2. Replaced by Yamada Saku on December 1, 1918.